I SHOULD KNOW THAT:

GREAT BRITAIN

Also by the same author:

I Used to Know That: History

Bad History: How We Got the Past Wrong

A History of the World in Bite-Sized Chunks

I SHOULD KNOW THAT:

GREAT BRITAIN

EVERYTHING YOU REALLY SHOULD KNOW ABOUT GB

EMMA MARRIOTT

Michael O'Mara Books Limited

This paperback edition first published in 2015

First published in Great Britain in 2013 by
Michael O'Mara Books Limited
9 Lion Yard
Tremadoc Road
London SW4 7NQ

A CIP catalogue record for this book is available from the British Library.

Papers used by Michael O'Mara Books Limited are natural, recyclable
products made from wood grown in sustainable forests. The
manufacturing processes conform to the environmental regulations of
the country of origin.

ISBN: 978-1-78243-431-3 in paperback print format
ISBN: 978-1-78243-066-7 in hardback print format
ISBN: 978-1-78243-163-3 in ebook format

1 2 3 4 5 6 7 8 9 10

Cover design by James Empringham
Illustrations by Siaron Hughes
Designed and typeset by K.DESIGN, Winscombe, Somerset

Printed and bound by CPI Group (UK) Ltd, Croydon, CR0 4YY

www.mombooks.com

CONTENTS

INTRODUCTION

'Political language … is designed to make lies sound truthful and murder respectable, and to give an appearance of solidity to pure wind.'

GEORGE ORWELL IN 'SHOOTING AN ELEPHANT' (1950).

In his critique of political prose, Orwell's argument was that politicians use vague language to obfuscate the truth. And he's right: politicians and their like are masters of evasiveness, wriggling out of tricky questions by hastily changing the subject or by delivering an incomprehensible stew of an answer bubbling with political jargon and gobbledegook. Often, they might also say something they really shouldn't or get their facts wrong, as admittedly we all do, but their errors, omissions, or off-the-cuff remarks can prove their undoing when they are made in full public glare.

British Prime Minister David Cameron was caught very publicly unaware when he struggled to answer a few 'dumb American questions' thrown at him by David Letterman when he appeared on the US host's chat show in September 2012. In doing so, Cameron guessed (wrongly) that Edward Elgar had composed 'Rule, Britannia!' and admitted to not knowing the literal translation of 'Magna Carta'. (To redeem himself, he did provide the correct date and place of the signing of the Magna Carta, succinctly explaining its significance in British political history and the evolution of democracy. See page 40.) Despite this, and knowing that the show aired to millions of US viewers, Cameron quipped, 'This is bad, I have ended my career on your show tonight.'

To add to Mr Cameron's embarrassment, the questions he failed to answer were of the type found in the 'Life in the United Kingdom' test, which must be taken by immigrants seeking British citizenship or permanent residency in the UK. Made up of twenty-four multiple-choice questions, the examination tests knowledge of the English language as well as important aspects of British life, its society, government, employment and values. It also includes a fairly heavy dose of British history, ranging from the Stone Age to the coalition government and beyond.

While the average pass rate for candidates seeking residency in the UK is a pretty impressive 70 per cent, it's clear that the vast majority of us Brits would struggle with many of the test's quite tricky (and, some have argued, irrelevant) questions. How many people, I wonder, could outline the powers of the devolved governments of

Scotland, Wales and Northern Ireland? Or summarize the events of the Wars of the Roses? Or know who can and cannot stand as an MP in Britain? And if asked to define the difference between the European Commission, European Council, and the Council of Ministers, I'm guessing that most Brits would break out in a cold sweat.

Nonetheless, this is the kind of information that all of us should really know about, much of which is provided in this book, with an outline of key events in British history (illustrious or not), the geography of the isles and the ever-changing make-up of British society, the country's laws and system of government, as well as its cultural pursuits and achievements. The book touches on the kind of information covered in the Life in the UK test but doesn't slavishly adhere to it, including extra bits of ephemera (like top-ten accidents in the garden or slang terms for Brits) that may not quite fit the remit set by the British Home Office.

And to enliven all the facts and stats, we've liberally sprinkled in some of the dumbest quotes, blunders and misfires from politicians, officials and their ilk, just so you know you're not alone in your ignorance. Luckily for us, they didn't follow the advice of fellow MP Norman Tebbit, who once said, 'Far better to keep your mouth shut and let everyone think you're stupid than open it and remove all doubt.'

EMMA MARRIOTT

'BRITAIN IS A WORLD BY ITSELF': IDENTITY

From the country's flags and patron saints to its rousing national anthems and the affectionate (and not so affectionate) names by which its inhabitants are sometimes known, the identifying aspects of the UK are plentiful.

UNITED KINGDOM OR GREAT BRITAIN?

Britain's official title today is the United Kingdom of Great Britain and Northern Ireland. However, it has not always been so. In 1707, Great Britain, which comprised England, Scotland and Wales, was formed by the political union of England and Scotland under the Acts of Union. In 1801, Great Britain merged with Ireland to create the United

Shetland Islands

Hebrides

Isle of Man

Anglesey

Isle of Wight

Isles of Scilly

Channel Islands

Kingdom of Great Britain and Ireland, and in 1922 the name changed to the United Kingdom of Great Britain and Northern Ireland, when most of Ireland seceded from the Union.

'As Secretary of State for Ireland ...' Peter Mandelson misses out a crucial word in his opening statement to the House of Commons in October 1999 after taking up his post of Northern Ireland Secretary of State.

Smaller islands off the British mainland such as the Isle of Wight, Anglesey and the Isles of Scilly, Shetlands and Hebrides form part of the British political union. The Channel Islands and the Isle of Man are not part of the United Kingdom. They are self-governing British crown dependencies with their own legal systems and legislatures, although the British government is responsible for their foreign relations and defence. Following devolution (see page 168), Scotland, Wales and Northern Ireland have developed their own administrations that are responsible for many domestic policy issues.

The name 'Britain' derives from the Roman name for the British Isles, *Britannia* (land of the Britons). The much older Celtic name *Albion* is still sometimes used today as a poetic reference to the British Isles. *Alba*, derived from *Albion*, is also the Gaelic name for Scotland (*Albain* in Irish and *Alban* in Welsh).

MAJOR'S VISION

'Fifty years on from now, Britain will still be the country of long shadows on country [cricket] grounds, warm beer, invincible green suburbs, dog lovers and pool fillers and old maids cycling to Holy Communion through the morning mist.'

THEN BRITISH PRIME MINISTER JOHN MAJOR IN A SPEECH TO THE CONSERVATIVE GROUP FOR EUROPE ON 22 APRIL 1993.

John Major's aim with this somewhat fanciful image of Great Britain was to convince the Conservative Party that he could defend the country when negotiating with the European Union. Satirists and the like responded with derision, to which he answered that he had simply 'quoted some poetry ... to illustrate that the essential characteristics of our country would never be lost by a deepening relationship with the European Union'. Major had possibly never read the original source as some of the words concerning the 'old maids' were in fact borrowed from George Orwell's essay, 'The Lion and the Unicorn', a socialist call to arms and vision of wartime Britain. Orwell also wrote of 'the crowds in the big towns with their mild knobby faces, their bad teeth', which was conveniently omitted from Major's speech.

SLANG TERMS FOR BRITS

If there's one thing Brits are known for, it's having a good sense of humour. Which is just as well considering some of the name-calling that has gone on over the years ...

Limey: a somewhat dated North American term, originally referring to British sailors who were given rations of lime juice to prevent scurvy. It is not (as some think) derived from the cockney phrase 'Cor, blimey', the contracted form of 'God blind me!'.

Pom or Pommy: used in Australia, New Zealand and South Africa. The origin is unknown, although the strongest theory is that it's a contraction of 'pomegranate', which was once Australian rhyming slang for immigrant.

Rosbif: a French term referring to the British national cuisine of roast beef but also subsequently to the British themselves. In Portugal, 'bife' also refers to the British, with 'bifa' referring to British female tourists.

Sassenach: used by the Scots and Irish to describe the English. The term is derived from the Scottish Gaelic for 'Saxon'.

Les goddams: a historic term of abuse coined by the French to denote the English, who were notorious for frequent swearing (God Damn!) during the Hundred Years War (1337–1453).

Taffy: a derogatory term for a Welshman, made popular by the English nursery rhyme, 'Taffy Was a Welshman'. The origin is unknown, although it may be a merging of the Cardiff river Taff and the common Welsh name 'Dafydd'.

Jock: refers to the Scots. Jock is a Scottish derivation of the forename John.

THE UNION JACK

The national flag of the United Kingdom is popularly known as the Union Jack. (The origin of the word 'jack' may be derived from Charles II's proclamation that the Union flag be flown only by the Royal Navy as a jack, a small flag.) It is a composite of three individual flags: the red St George's cross of England, the red diagonal cross (saltire) of Saint Patrick, and the white saltire of St Andrew.

The current flag dates back to 1801, after the union of Great Britain with Ireland. Wales was not originally recognized on the Union flag because, following its annexation by Edward I in 1284, it was deemed part of the Kingdom of England.

FLYING THE FLAG

As the Union Jack is not symmetrical, there is a right way and a wrong way to fly it. The thick white parts of the diagonal cross nearest the flagpole should be placed above the thinner white parts. The difference is subtle, which means the flag is frequently flown incorrectly.

On 3 February 2009, a table top version of the flag was flown upside down at a trade agreement ceremony involving Chinese premier Wen Jiabao, the then British Prime Minister Gordon Brown and Trade Secretary Lord Mandelson. Historically, flying the flag upside down was seen as a signal of distress, and Tory MP Andrew Rosindell called it 'an unbelievable flaw in protocol for Number Ten.' In a statement that followed, Downing Street said, 'It is regrettable that, on this occasion, the Union flag was not displayed correctly. We have looked into how this happened and have taken steps to ensure it is correctly displayed at all times in the future.'

NATIONAL EMBLEMS

From roses and thistles to dragons and bulldogs, the crests of the British Isles run the gamut.

ROSE

The Tudor rose is used as the symbol of England. Following the end of the Wars of the Roses, Tudor king Henry VII conjoined the white rose of York and red rose of Lancaster to create the Tudor rose.

THREE LIONS

They feature on the Royal Arms of England, symbolizing England and all its monarchs. Royal emblems featuring lions were first used by William the Conqueror (1066–1154) and have continued to appear on the royal arms of England, as well as more recently on the badge of the England national football team and the British £1 coin.

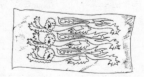

THISTLE

This has been the national symbol of Scotland since the reign of Scottish king Alexander III (1249–86). Legend has it that Vikings, attempting to invade by stealth, mistakenly alerted the Scots to their presence when one barefoot Viking stepped upon a thistle. He cried out in pain, which enabled the Scots to repel their invaders.

LEEK AND DAFFODIL

The national emblems of Wales and worn on St David's Day (see page 189). An early Welsh king, King Cadwaladr of Gwynedd (c. 655–82) is said to have ordered his soldiers to wear leeks on their helmets in a battle with the Saxons; Shakespeare in *Henry V* refers to the 'ancient tradition' of wearing a leek. Little is known about the daffodil's association with Wales – it may have become a popular emblem because it shares the same Welsh name as leek, *ceninen*.

THE WELSH DRAGON

This appears in red on the flag of Wales along with the colours of green and white. The dragon has been associated with Wales for centuries but the origin behind its adoption is obscure. Ancient Celtic and Romano-British leaders are said to have used the dragon as a battle standard, as did Welsh prince Owain Glyndŵr in 1400 during his revolts against English occupation in Wales. The dragon formed part of the Tudor royal arms to signify their Welsh descent. Later, the Tudor colours of green and white were added. The flag was only granted official status in 1959 and currently flies from the Welsh Assembly building in Cardiff and the Wales office in Whitehall.

JOHN BULL

The personification of England and the English character, Bull was invented by the Scottish political satirist John Arbuthnot in 1712, and soon became a popular caricature in eighteenth-century political writings. His image evolved in the nineteenth century into a jovial, everyman farmer

 figure with a bulldog at his heel, Union Jack waistcoat and a squat top hat. By the time of the Second World War, British Prime Minister Winston Churchill seemed to embody the characteristics of both John Bull and a bulldog.

'The nose of the bulldog has been slanted backwards so he can breathe without letting go.'

THEN PRIME MINISTER WINSTON CHURCHILL (1874–1965) TO THE BRITISH PEOPLE DURING THE SECOND WORLD WAR.

NATIONAL ANTHEMS

Patriotic and rousing, the national anthems of Great Britain conjure up images of a green and pleasant land.

'GOD SAVE THE QUEEN (OR KING)'

The national and royal anthem of Britain is 'God Save the Queen (or King)'. The song was first performed publicly in 1745 at the Theatre Royal in Drury Lane, London, after a performance of the Ben Jonson play *The Alchemist*. The origin of the words and music is unknown, although a possible candidate is the poet, playwright and prolific songwriter Henry Carey (who suffered great poverty in his life, committing suicide in 1743). It is used as a national anthem for a number of Commonwealth countries (including Australia, Canada and New Zealand) and in other countries the melody is sung with different words, such as the American version, 'My country, 'tis of thee'. In general, only one verse is sung, although occasionally another two or three verses are added on.

'RULE, BRITANNIA!'

> US chat-show host David Letterman to British Prime Minister David Cameron: '"Rule Britannia!". Written by whom?' Cameron: 'You're testing me there … Elgar, I'll go for Elgar.'
>
> *LATE SHOW WITH DAVID LETTERMAN* ON 26 SEPTEMBER 2012.

A rousing British song, strongly associated with the Royal Navy, 'Rule, Britannia!' is based on a poem of the same name written in 1740 by Scottish poet and playwright James Thomson (1700–48), and set to music by leading theatre composer Thomas Arne (1710–78).

Mr Cameron's confusion with Elgar might have been because the theme of Elgar's *Enigma Variations* is thought to have been based partly on the melody of 'Rule Britannia's!' refrain, 'never will be slaves' (more often than not corrupted to 'never, never, never …'). Elgar also quotes the opening phrase of the song in *The Music Makers*.

'LAND OF HOPE AND GLORY'

In all likelihood, however, Mr Cameron simply confused 'Rule, Britannia!' with another patriotic song, 'Land of Hope and Glory'. This *was* written by English composer Edward Elgar in 1902, its refrain forming the 'trio' theme for his *Pomp and Circumstance March No 1*. With lyrics by the English writer A. C. Benson, the song was formerly sung by England at international rugby matches and by the England team at the Commonwealth games. The lyrics 'Wider still and wider shall thy bounds be set' refer to the extension of the British Empire and, possibly, the territorial gains made during the Second Boer War (1899–1902).

'JERUSALEM'

Often sung in churches (including the 2011 wedding of Prince William and Catherine Middleton), at the Labour Party conference and at meetings of the Women's Institute, 'Jerusalem' is another of Britain's patriotic songs. Its words derive from William Blake's (1757–1827) poem, 'And did those feet in ancient time', and its music was written by the English composer Sir Hubert Parry in 1916 and orchestrated by Elgar in 1922. The poem is based on a fanciful story that Jesus visited England during his 'lost years'. The poem's phrases 'dark Satanic mills', 'chariot of fire' and 'green and pleasant land' are now strongly associated with the English identity and inspired several segments of the opening ceremony of the 2012 London Olympic Games.

'FLOWER OF SCOTLAND'

Like England, Scotland doesn't have an official national anthem but 'Flower of Scotland' frequently fulfils this role, along with 'Scotland the Brave' and 'Scots Wha Hae'. It's a relative newcomer, written in 1967 by the Scottish folk musician Roy Williamson, and describes Robert the Bruce's victory over the English at the Battle of Bannockburn in 1314 (see page 42).

'HEN WLAD FY NHADAU'

Often translated as 'Land of my Fathers', 'Hen Wlad Fy Nhadau' is the Welsh national anthem. The Welsh weaver and poet Evan James wrote the lyrics in 1856 and his son James James wrote the music in the same year.

'LONDONDERRY AIR'

Although 'God Save the Queen (or King)' is the national anthem of Northern Ireland, 'Londonderry Air' is often sung as an alternative. It is also the victory anthem for Northern Ireland at the Commonwealth Games. The origin of the tune is unknown, and it has been sung with many lyrics, the most popular of which are 'Danny Boy', which was written by English lawyer Frederic Edward Weatherly (1848–1929), who never set foot in Northern Ireland and who published the revised version in 1913.

BY HEART

'Before dinner, we [he and his then secretary Ffion Jenkins] thought I had better learn the Welsh national anthem.'

WILLIAM HAGUE

In 1995, William Hague, newly appointed Secretary of State for Wales, made sure he learnt the words of the Welsh national anthem prior to attending the Royal National Eisteddfod of Wales. He was keen not to repeat the excruciatingly embarrassing mistake of his predecessor, John Redwood, who, two years earlier in full public glare, had unconvincingly mouthed the words of the Welsh national anthem.

ICONS OF BRITAIN

Spanning the breadth of the country, the following iconic emblems of Britain encompass its unique character.

THE WHITE CLIFFS OF DOVER

The white cliffs of Dover, which face continental Europe at the narrowest point of the English Channel, are intricately linked with the history of Britain. Standing up to 300 feet

(90 metres) high, they form a symbolic guard against invasion and provide a reassuring sight to returning travellers. The cliffs have been immortalized in art, literature and song, and most famously in the popular Second World War song '(There'll Be Bluebirds Over) The White Cliffs of Dover' sung by 'The Forces' Sweetheart' Dame Vera Lynn. The composer Walter Kent and lyricist Nat Burton, who wrote the song in 1941, were both American, as are bluebirds, which have never flown over the white cliffs of Dover.

THE ROUTEMASTER BUS

'Only some ghastly, dehumanized moron would want to get rid of the Routemaster.'

KEN LIVINGSTONE, MAYOR OF LONDON, 2001. BY 2005,
HE HAD THEM ALL PHASED OUT.

The distinctive double-decker red bus, known as the Routemaster, is one of London's most famous symbols and a British design icon widely recognized overseas. Despite its popularity, the original Routemaster bus was retired from service in London in 2005 by the then Mayor of London Ken Livingstone as a result of new government legislation, which required full accessibility for wheelchair users. The iconic bus, with its open platform at the back to allow passengers to hop on and off at any time, was first introduced to the London streets by London Transport in 1956, and saw continuous service until 2005. A new version of the Routemaster bus, sometimes known as the Boris Bus (named after Livingstone's successor, Boris Johnson, who campaigned for and introduced them) first entered service on 27 February 2012, with eight of the new buses running on route 38 (Victoria to Clapton Pond in Hackney). Unlike its predecessor, the bus allows passengers to alight at the front end and in the middle, but retains the pole and platform at the rear to allow passengers to hop on and off.

THE ANGEL OF THE NORTH

Standing at an impressive 20 metres high and with a wingspan of 54 metres, the *Angel of the North* is Britain's largest sculpture. Designed by Turner prize-winning artist Antony Gormley, the vast steel structure is positioned at the top of a hill in Gateshead, north-east England, overlooking the A1. When the sculpture was erected in 1998 it aroused some controversy, with local councillor Martin Callanan particularly vocal in his opposition. Known locally as the 'Gateshead Flasher', the angel has since become a key landmark for north-east England and, with almost 33 million people passing by in trains and cars every year, one of the most viewed artworks in the world.

STONEHENGE

Built in stages from 3000 BC, Stonehenge is Europe's most famous prehistoric monument and is listed by UNESCO as a World Heritage Site. Its circular setting of large standing stones are surrounded by scores of burial mounds on the Salisbury Plain, Wiltshire. Little is known about the rituals that were performed at Stonehenge but its alignment of stones suggest that it was connected with the passage of the sun and the passing of the seasons. Despite popular belief, the stones were not built by Iron Age druids.

SCOTTISH CLANS AND TARTAN

The tribal groups of the Scottish Highlands, dating back to the twelfth century, are known as clans (from the Gaelic meaning 'family'). The clan's patriarch was known as a chief and all members of the clan bore his surname, although they were not necessarily related by blood. Each clan had its own tartan patterns (established mainly in the nineteenth century), clan crest and plant associated with its territory (such as the Scots pine worn by the MacGregors of Argyll), which were displayed on the bonnet. The Battle of Culloden in 1746 (see page 53) led to the end of the clan system, with clan lands forfeited to the Crown and the wearing of tartan banned for 100 years. The clan system exists now only in name but they remain a strong source of pride for many Scots.

THE GREENWICH MERIDIAN

'Tourists go home with the photographs showing them with one foot in the northern hemisphere and one in the southern.'

FORMER SOCIAL DEMOCRATIC PARTY MP ROSIE BARNES IN
HER MAIDEN SPEECH TO THE HOUSE OF COMMONS, 1987,
REFERRING TO THE PRIME MERIDIAN IN THE ROYAL
OBSERVATORY OF HER CONSTITUENCY GREENWICH.

The Prime Meridian is housed in the Royal Observatory in Greenwich, London, and it divides the *eastern* and *western* hemispheres of the world. Every place on earth is measured in terms of its distance east or west from this line. It's the equator that divides the northern and southern hemispheres, and this is a long way from Greenwich.

Since 1884, the Prime Meridian has also served as the reference line for Greenwich Mean Time, the time standard for the world and from which the twenty-four-hour time zones grew. GMT – with slight refinements to keep it in time with atomic clocks – is known as Coordinated Universal Time and is still the world's time standard.

GIANT'S CAUSEWAY

The most popular tourist attraction in Northern Ireland (and the fourth greatest natural wonder in the UK) is the Giant's Causeway. Located in County Antrim, on the north-east coastline of Northern Ireland, 40,000 basalt (volcanic rock) columns, many of them hexagonal, stretch out to sea to form a strange landscape that has captivated locals and visitors for centuries. Legend tells of an Irish giant Finn MacCool creating the causeway some 2,000 years ago. Science, however, tells us that the causeway was formed some 50 to 60 million years ago when Antrim was subject to intense volcanic activity caused by the tectonic plates of Europe and North America moving apart. Magma deep inside the earth spewed up through cracks to form a lava plateau, which cooled rapidly, leaving pillar-like structures in its wake.

ST DAVID'S, WALES

The largest cathedral in Wales is situated in Britain's smallest city, St David's in Pembrokeshire, south-west Wales. St David, a Welsh native and bishop during the sixth century, founded a monastic settlement at this location in AD 550. He was later named as the patron saint of Wales and his shrine at St David's became a popular place of pilgrimage for Christians throughout the Middle Ages (three visits here equalled one to Jerusalem). The date of St David's death is 1 March AD 589, and is commemorated throughout Wales.

ST GEORGE

The patron saint of England, St George is a somewhat mysterious character. Little is known about the man himself, other than he was a soldier of noble birth who probably never set foot in England, and who was put to death under the Roman Emperor Diocletian on 23 April AD 303, possibly for protesting against the persecution of Christians. Stories of St George circulated during the Crusades and Richard I put his army under the protection of St George during his Palestine campaign in 1191–2. The legend of George slaying a dragon may be an allegory of the persecution of Diocletian or a Christianized version of the Greek legend of Perseus, who is said to have rescued the virgin Andromeda from a sea monster. It also owes much to the culture of chivalry in the High Middle Ages. By the end of the fourteenth century, St George had become acknowledged as the patron saint of England and, since 1222, 23 April has been known as St George's Day.

AN AWARD FOR EXCELLENCE

In 1940, when Britain was subject to mass bombings by Germany, George VI introduced the George Cross for acts of heroism. Usually given to civilians, the award is a silver cross and bears St George slaying a dragon on one side, with the inscription 'For Gallantry'.

ST ANDREW

St Andrew's Day, in commemoration of the patron saint of Scotland, is celebrated by Scots on 30 November. Little is known about St Andrew himself, other than he was born in the early first century AD in Galilee; he and his elder brother Simon Peter were both fishermen and both became apostles of Jesus. He is said to have been crucified by the Romans in Patras, southern Greece, by being bound to a diagonal cross, the basis of the St Andrew's saltire as featured on the Scottish flag. Andrew became the patron saint of Scotland in the middle of the tenth century, and several legends state that his relics were taken from Constantinople to St Andrews on the east coast of Scotland. St Andrews evolved into a medieval place of pilgrimage and a religious centre of Scotland. Today St Andrews is more of a Mecca for golfers, as well as for students attending its university.

ST PATRICK

St Patrick is the patron saint of the Republic of Ireland and Northern Ireland, and on 17 March, the anniversary of his death, St Patrick's Day is celebrated around the world. He was born in c. AD 387 somewhere on mainland Britain (location unknown), captured by Irish marauders at the age of sixteen and taken to Ireland as a slave, during which time 'he turned with fervour to his faith'. Six years later, he escaped to Britain, trained as a priest and returned to Ireland in AD 433, where he brought the message of Christianity to much of the country.

'WHAT'S PAST IS PROLOGUE': HISTORY

Britain's history is rich and illustrious, peppered by battles, war, triumphs and disasters. It is impossible to understand our current world without delving into the country's fascinating past.

'Just because Europe adopts the euro is no reason why we should! We have a much older history!'

MARGARET THATCHER, ELECTION CAMPAIGN, MAY 2001

PREHISTORIC BRITAIN

6000–5000 BC The British Isles separates from the European mainland as melting ice causes the English Channel to form.

4000 BC Farming is introduced and Stone Age settlements grow. Skara Brae in the Orkney Islands, to the north of Scotland, is the best-preserved prehistoric village in northern Europe.

3000–1520 BC Stonehenge (see page 26), along with other stone circles and burial mounds, built around Britain.

2500 BC The Bronze Age begins as people start to make things from copper, gold and bronze.

650 BC The Celts, many from Belgic Gaul, bring to Britain the technique for smelting iron, ushering in the Iron Age. Hilltop forts are built.

ROMAN BRITAIN

55 and 54 BC Julius Caesar lands in Britain but the Roman army withdraws.

AD 43 The Roman Emperor Claudius successfully invades Britain, which becomes part of the Roman Empire.

AD 61 Queen Boadicea of the British Iceni tribe leads an uprising against Roman rule, laying waste to St Albans,

Colchester and London. The Romans almost lose their grip on Britain but the superior military discipline of their army ultimately defeats the uprising.

CAPITAL GAINS

Camulodunum (Colchester) was the first provincial Roman capital of Britannia (Britain). It was destroyed during Boadicea's rebellion, and some time after that Londinium (London) became the capital, its situation on the Thames more convenient for trade.

AD 69–96 Romans conquer Wales and the north of England.

AD 78–84 The Gallo-Roman general Gnaeus Julius Agricola advances into Scotland, then retreats.

AD 122–130 Roman Emperor Hadrian begins to build a wall on the border of Scotland.

AD 140–3 Romans occupy southern Scotland and build the Antonine Wall to mark their frontier.

THE BORDERLINE

At 118 km (73 miles) long, Hadrian's Wall represented the largest structure in the Roman Empire. It ran from Wallsend-on-Tyne in the east to Bowness on the Solway Firth in the west. The Antonine Wall ran across the central belt of Scotland between the Firth of Forth and Firth of Clyde. At 59 km (37 miles) long, much of the wall has been destroyed and its remains are less visible than Hadrian's Wall.

c. 180 Tribes in northern Britain rebel against the Romans.

200 onwards The Romans face increasing attacks from Picts and Scots.

211–12 Roman Emperor Caracalla, son of Septimius Severus, divides Britain into two provinces, with governors at London and York.

260–274 Britain, along with Gaul, Spain and lower Germany, splits from Rome to form the Gallic Empire.

287–293 Carausius, commander of the Roman British Fleet, revolts and rules Britain as Emperor.

296 The Roman authorities regain control of Britain.

360s The Saxons, composed of Germanic-speaking tribes, begin to raid Britain.

410 The Romans withdraw from Britain.

'Clearly the future is still to come.'

PETER BROOKE, CONSERVATIVE MP, 1986.

ANGLO-SAXON AND VIKING BRITAIN

430 Ninian becomes the first Christian missionary in Scotland.

449 onwards Angles and Saxons, tribes from northern Europe, begin to invade and settle in the south and east of Britain. From the 550s, Anglo-Saxons set up seven kingdoms and begin pushing westward, although Scotland and much of what is now Wales remains free of Anglo-Saxon rule.

500s Christianity is spread by St Patrick, who arrives in Ireland from Britain in the 430s; St David, who founds a monastery in Wales in the 550s; St Columba, who arrives in Scotland from Ireland in the 560s; and St Augustine, who is sent from Rome to convert the English in 597.

731 Bede completes his *Ecclesiastical History of the English People*, a work of genuine scholarship.

757–96 King Offa of Mercia (now the Midlands) dominates much of southern England. He constructs an earth wall marking the border between Mercia and Wales, known as Offa's Dyke.

789 The Vikings, a seafaring people from Denmark and Norway, begin to land in the south of England. By 871 the Vikings have conquered large parts of the north and east of England, and parts of Ireland.

843 Kenneth MacAlpine, king of Dalriada, an over-kingdom on the western coast of Scotland and in parts of Ulster, drives out the Vikings and becomes king of all Scotland. Rhodri Mawr, king of Gwynedd in Wales (844–78), also fights off Viking invaders and comes to rule most of Wales.

THE GREATEST

Alfred the Great (849–99) King of Wessex is the only English king to have been given the moniker 'Great'. Having defended his kingdom from invading Vikings, he also established an efficient administration. His reign also oversaw a history of English people, *The Anglo-Saxon Chronicle*, which is one of the best sources for information on the period.

STEMMING THE TIDE

'I sometimes feel like King Canute. Yes, indeed. Just like King Canute with his finger in the dyke.'

CONSERVATIVE MP NIRJ DEVA, MARCH 2001.

In 2011, Labour MP Frank Field warned David Cameron to 'stop being King Canute' if he wanted to avoid being 'overwhelmed by the incoming tide of local authority cuts'.

King Canute, the Danish king who ruled England from 1017 to 1035, is frequently quoted by politicians to denote deluded arrogance. In fact, the story is generally misrepresented – Canute is said to have set his throne by the sea shore and commanded the tide to halt in a bid to prove to his courtiers that he *couldn't* command the waves, saying, 'Let all men know how empty and worthless is the power of kings, for there is none worthy of thy name, but He whom heaven, earth, and sea obey by eternal laws.'

Canute also never put his finger in a dyke – Nirj Deva has simply got her stories horribly confused. It was a novel entitled *Hans Brinker, or The Silver Skates* (1865), that told the story of a little Dutch boy who saves his country by plugging a dyke with his finger.

878 King Alfred defeats the Vikings at Edington and in 886 captures London and divides England into two halves: the north, central and east remain under Danish rule, known as the Danelaw, and the rest of England remains under Saxon control.

THE NORMANS AND THE MIDDLE AGES

1066 William of Normandy defeats King Harold of England at the Battle of Hastings. (Harold's gruesome death is depicted in the Bayeux Tapestry with an arrow piercing the king's eye.) The Normans go on to conquer Wales and parts of Scotland and Ireland, and they replace the Anglo-Saxons as the ruling class of England. The early Norman kings and nobility hold lands on both sides of the Channel, and are predominantly French-speaking. Gradually the two languages of Norman French and Anglo-Saxon combine to become one English language, and by 1400 English is the preferred language of Parliament and the royal court.

1086 William I ('the Conqueror') commissions for tax purposes a comprehensive survey of property and land in his conquered territory, later nicknamed the Domesday Book, in reference to God's last day of judgement.

ON LOAN

The Normans brought with them a particularly efficient form of feudalism, in which the king leased land to religious institutions or powerful lords in return for loyalty or military service. These lands were divided into manors or estates for which lesser nobles or tenants were obliged to pay homage. At the bottom of the heap was a class of bonded peasant, known as serfs or villeins, who lived entirely under the jurisdiction of their master. Out of this system grew fortified castles built by lords to defend their realms.

1189–99 Richard I (better known as 'the Lionheart') joins France in the Crusades (religious wars waged by Christendom against Muslim Turks in the Middle East). He succeeds in recapturing the city of Acre (now in Israel) from the Muslim Turks but fails to take Jerusalem.

1215 The Magna Carta (Latin for 'Great Charter') was a document drawn up by feudal barons in England in a bid to protect their privileges and limit the king's powers. King John, an unpopular ruler who had lost vast territories in France and continually squeezed his subjects for tax, was forced to agree to the terms of the document at Runnymede (situated on the River Thames in Surrey). Arguably Britain's most famous legal document, the Magna Carta proclaims the rights and liberties of individual subjects and is often considered to be an early step in the evolution of constitutional law in Britain and in English-speaking countries across the world. In spite of its fame, however, only three of its sixty-three clauses are still recognized by English law.

> Prime Minister David Cameron on *Late Show with David Letterman* is questioned on the literal translation of 'Magna Carta':
> Cameron: 'Again, you're testing me.'
> Letterman: 'It would be good if you knew this.'

1282–3 Edward I conquers Wales, where he builds huge castles, such as those at Caernarfon and Conwy, to consolidate his power. In 1296 Edward invades Scotland but the Scots resist.

1295 Edward I calls the Model Parliament, the first representative parliament, summoning churchmen and nobles and issuing orders for the election of two knight representatives from each county and two burgesses from each town.

1297 William Wallace leads the Scots to victory against Edward I at the Battle of Stirling Bridge, part of the First War of Scottish Independence. However, in 1304 Edward defeats the Scots and William Wallace is executed.

41

1314   Robert the Bruce, king of the Scots, leads a decisive victory against the English at the Battle of Bannockburn. England fails to conquer Scotland.

1337   Continual friction between France and England over French territories leads to a series of wars known as the Hundred Years War (which actually lasts 116 years). In 1346 Edward III (aided by his son Edward, dubbed the Black Prince, after the colour of his armour) defeats the French at the Battle of Crécy.

1348   The Black Death, a virulent and terrifying form of bubonic and pneumonic plague, arrives in Britain and kills roughly one-third of the population. Outbreaks occur over the next thirty years, leading to a sharp decline in population. Labour shortages ensue, which increases the bargaining power of the peasants and leads to a fragmentation of the feudal system (see page 40).

1381   The introduction of the poll tax triggers the Peasants' Revolt, in which an army of villagers and townsmen from Kent and Essex, under the leadership of Wat Tyler, Jack Straw and John Ball, march on London. There they run riot, murder the Archbishop of Canterbury and capture the Tower of London. The young King Richard II eventually executes the ringleaders of the uprising.

1415   Henry V defeats the French at the Battle of Agincourt, a major victory during the Hundred Years' War.

'WE FEW, WE HAPPY FEW'

The defeat of the French at the Battle of Agincourt, with the French outnumbering the English army by approximately 2:1, has gone down in the annals of British history as a heroic victory. Immortalized in Shakespeare's *Henry V*, the words 'We few, we happy few, we band of brothers' enshrined the belief that the English do best when they are outnumbered.

The defeat of the Spanish Armada by a small fleet of English ships in 1588 was again presented as a victory against all the odds, a conviction used to great effect by Winston Churchill in a House of Commons speech several centuries later, in 1940, when he referred to the skill and courage of British airmen during the Second World War: 'Never in the field of human conflict was so much owed by so many to so few.'

1477 The first printed book is published by William Caxton.

1483 Richard III becomes king. His reign is mired in controversy, many believing he imprisoned his two nephews, the twelve-year-old Edward V and his brother Richard, in the Tower of London and then murdered them, giving rise to the legend of the 'Princes in the Tower'.

1485 The Battle of Bosworth Field marks the death of Richard III. His defeat at the hands of Henry VII marks a decisive victory in the Wars of the Roses and the ushering in of the Tudor dynasty.

THE WARS OF THE ROSES

Beginning in 1455, the Wars of the Roses were a series of civil battles fought between the leading English dynasties, the House of Lancaster (represented in heraldry by the red rose) and the House of York (represented by the white rose). In 1486, Richard III's successor, Henry VII of the House of Lancaster, married Elizabeth of the House of York, thereby uniting the two families and merging the red and white roses to create the new emblem: the Tudor rose.

THE TUDORS AND STUARTS

1509 Henry VII dies and his son Henry VIII takes the throne.

1513 The English defeat the Scots at the Battle of Flodden, killing Scottish King James IV.

DIVORCED, BEHEADED, DIED ...

Pity the poor wives of Henry VIII.

Catherine of Aragon (queen 1509–33) Spanish princess and widow of Henry's brother, Arthur. Their marriage bore one child, Mary, and ended in divorce.

Anne Boleyn (queen 1533–6) A member of court circles, her marriage to Henry resulted in a daughter, Elizabeth. Anne Bolyen was beheaded on charges of adultery.

Jane Seymour (queen 1536–7) Gave birth to a male heir, Edward, but she died not long afterwards.

Anne of Cleves (queen Jan to July 1540) Apparently disappointed by her appearance, Henry had the marriage annulled after only six months.

Catherine Howard (queen 1540–1) Married swiftly following Henry's annulment from Anne. Catherine was beheaded a year later on grounds of adultery.

Katherine Parr (queen 1543–7) Twice-married Parr became Henry's wife until his death in 1547. She is England's most married queen, going on to marry Thomas Seymour six months after Henry's death.

1527 Having failed to produce a male heir, Henry VIII applies to Pope Clement VII for an annulment of his marriage to his first wife, Catherine of Aragon (whom he had married in 1509).

1533–4 When the pope refuses, Henry, with the help of his chief adviser, Thomas Cromwell, severs the English Church from Rome. As the Church's new supreme head, Henry presses on with his divorce and goes on to marry another five times.

1536 The Laws in Wales Act sees the union of England and Wales and the imposition, by Henry, of English law on Wales.

1541 Henry declares himself King of Ireland and in 1542 establishes a union between the Crowns, stating that anyone who becomes King of England will also become King of Ireland. Many Irish resent the claims of the English monarchy and refuse to sever ties with Rome.

1542 James V of Scotland invades England but is defeated at the Battle of Solway Moss.

1542 Six-day-old Mary Stuart, 'Queen of Scots', succeeds the Scottish throne, although she spends most of her childhood in France, marrying the Dauphin of France in 1558. In 1567 she is forced to abdicate the Scottish throne in favour of her Protestant son James VI of Scotland, and she flees to England. Perceived by many English Catholics as the legitimate sovereign of England, Mary is imprisoned in various great houses by her cousin Elizabeth I and is eventually executed in 1587.

1547 Nine-year-old Edward VI is crowned King of England and Ireland. During his reign, a series of reforms establishes Protestantism.

1553 Dying aged just fifteen, Edward is succeeded by his cousin Lady Jane Grey for a mere nine days before his half-sister Mary I succeeds in taking the throne. Mary, a devout Catholic, sets about reversing her brother's Protestant reforms and burns almost 300 'heretics', earning her the nickname 'Bloody Mary'.

1558 Elizabeth I becomes queen. Her unmarried status develops into a cult of virginity, depicted by poets and artists as the Virgin Queen. She establishes a moderate form of Protestantism and the Church of England as we know it today.

1560 The Scottish Parliament votes in Protestantism as the official religion.

1588 Elizabeth I defeats the vast fleet of the Spanish Armada, thwarting Spanish attempts to conquer England.

'I know I have the body of a weak and feeble woman, but I have the heart and stomach of a king, and a king of England too ...'

QUEEN ELIZABETH I SPEAKS TO THE TROOPS AT TILBURY ON THE APPROACH OF THE ARMADA.

1603 Scottish King James VI becomes James I of England, Wales and Ireland. In 1611 a new translation of the Bible is completed, known as the King James Bible, which is still used in many Protestant churches today.

1605 The Gunpowder Plot, organized by a group of English Catholics to blow up Parliament and assassinate James I of England (VI of Scotland), is thwarted.

1607 Jamestown, the first permanent English colony in North America, is founded in present-day Virginia, following the failed attempt of Sir Walter Raleigh (explorer, navigator and one of Queen Elizabeth's favourite courtiers) to set up a colony there in 1584.

1620 Puritans on the *Mayflower* set sail from England to North America and found New England. Over the next century, English fleets sail across the Atlantic to set up a string of settlements on the eastern seaboard of North America, as well as in the West Indies.

GUNPOWDER, TREASON AND PLOT

Robert Catesby led a group of provincial Catholic plotters in a plan to blow up Parliament during the State Opening on 5 November 1605. The gang included Guy Fawkes, who was found by the authorities guarding thirty-six barrels of gunpowder in the House of Lords the night before the event. It's the custom in Britain to commemorate the failure of the Gunpowder Plot on 5 November (known as Guy Fawkes or Bonfire Night). Bonfires are lit, fireworks let off and traditionally (although less common now) children make 'guys' – grotesque effigies of Guy Fawkes – which are then placed atop the bonfire and burnt.

1625 Charles I inherits the throne of England, Wales, Ireland and Scotland. Like his father James I, Charles believes kings have a God-given right to rule. This sentiment, combined with his apparent support for High Church Anglicanism (which looked suspiciously Catholic) brings him into conflict with Parliament and Puritan (radical Protestant) ministers. Between 1629 and 1640 he establishes an autocratic 'Personal Rule' without calling Parliament.

49

1641   A violent rebellion in Ireland follows decades of disorder and resentment caused by royalty-endorsed settlements, known as 'plantations', in Ireland by English and Scottish Protestants. James I's mass plantation of Ulster results in the displacement of thousands of landless Irish, fails to make the Irish Protestant and shores up more resentment against the English. Plantations are renewed with force under Cromwell in the 1650s and again in the 1680s and 1690s, so that land ownership by Irish Catholics drops from 90 per cent in 1600 to less than 15 per cent in 1700.

1642–9   The English Civil War erupts between the Parliamentarians (the Roundheads) and the Royalists (the Cavaliers), ending in the victory of the former. Charles I's execution in 1649 leads to the establishment of a republic under Parliament's leading general, Oliver Cromwell. His rule comes to be known as the Commonwealth.

1660   Following Cromwell's death in 1658, Charles's son returns to the throne and is crowned Charles II. Britain's monarchy is reinstated.

1665 and 1666   Plague breaks out in London, followed by the Great Fire in 1666, which devastates much of the City of London. Many churches are destroyed, including St Paul's, which is rebuilt by leading architect Sir Christopher Wren.

1679 The Habeas Corpus Act of Parliament, which is still in force today, ensures that no one can be imprisoned unlawfully or detained without charge. Its literal translation means 'You have the body', a Latin term for a writ requiring a person to be brought before a judge or court to determine if that person's imprisonment is lawful.

1685 Catholic James II becomes king. The 'Glorious Revolution' of 1688 leads to Parliamentarians deposing James II in favour of Protestant rulers William III (previously William of Orange) and Mary II.

1690 In an attempt to regain the throne, James II, fighting with a combined Franco-Irish force, is defeated by William III at the Battle of the Boyne in Ireland. A turning point in British-Irish history, the battle is still commemorated today in Northern Ireland.

1702 Queen Anne ascends the throne.

1707 The Act of Union unites England, Scotland and Wales under one parliament.

1709 Abraham Darby works out how to produce sheet iron from coke (a pure form of coal), which means iron goods can be produced on a large scale – a vital element of the Industrial Revolution (see page 54).

RIGHT ON

In 1689, William and Mary signed the Bill of Rights, which, among other developments:

- Limited the power of the monarch and laid out certain basic rights of all people, such as the right to petition and for just treatment by the courts
- Established the rights of Parliament, which had to agree to tax rises and the administration of justice, and set out rules of freedom of speech in Parliament and the right of regular elections
- Stipulated that Roman Catholics should be excluded from the Crown

The Bill of Rights is seen as one of the most important documents in British history (and a model for the US Bill of Rights, in 1791). Along with documents such as the Magna Carta (see page 40), it forms part of Britain's uncodified constitution.

THE GEORGIANS AND VICTORIANS

1714 After the death of Queen Anne, George I of the House of Hanover (in what is now Germany) becomes king. In response, Jacobites attempt to depose George in favour of Anne's Catholic half-brother James, the Old Pretender.

ALL FOR ONE

The term Jacobite, from the Latin *Jacobus* for 'James', refers to supporters of the exiled James II and his descendants.

1720   The South Sea Bubble bursts, a securities fraud that sees frenzied speculation before its shares collapse, ruining many investors and disgracing a number of politicians. Scientist Sir Isaac Newton loses a fortune, lamenting, 'I can calculate the movement of the stars, but not the madness of men.'

1721   Robert Walpole is reappointed First Lord of the Treasury and Chancellor of the Exchequer, effectively becoming Britain's first prime minister (although the term is not used at the time).

1727   George II takes the throne.

1746   Jacobite claimant to the throne, Bonnie Prince Charlie (also known as Charles Edward Stuart, grandson of James II), is defeated at the Battle of Culloden. Jacobite casualties are heavy, as is the crackdown on Jacobitism and Highland culture (including Highland clans).

1760   George III becomes king.

1764 James Hargreaves invents the spinning jenny, which enables textile workers to spin eight threads at once. The mechanization of the textile industry, a key business for Britain, is further developed with Richard Arkwright's design of a water-powered spinning machine in 1769 and Edmund Cartwright's water-powered (and later steam-powered) loom in 1785. Developments in machinery along with the use of steam power help Britain to industrialize rapidly in the eighteenth and nineteenth centuries, mechanizing the manufacture of goods and agriculture, a process known as the Industrial Revolution.

1770 Captain James Cook lands in Botany Bay, Australia. In 1788, Port Jackson (later Sydney) is declared Britain's first penal settlement and over the next eighty years, 160,000 convicts are transported to new Australian colonies.

1775 Relations between the British government and its colonies in North America worsen (largely over Britain's attempts to tax the colonists without consent), leading to the American War of Independence. In 1776, Britain's thirteen colonies in America sign the Declaration of Independence and eventually defeat the British army, with the British recognizing the colony's independence in 1783.

1801 The Acts of Union unite the kingdom of Great Britain with the kingdom of Ireland to create the United Kingdom of Great Britain and Ireland.

1793–1815 A series of wars rage in Europe as various European coalitions fight against the French in an attempt to restore the French king to the throne (following the French Revolution) and to limit the aggressive expansion of Napoleon Bonaparte, who has become Emperor of France.

1805 British admiral Horatio Nelson destroys the combined French and Spanish fleet at the Battle of Trafalgar, during which he is mortally wounded.

KISS ME

Admiral Horatio Nelson (1758–1805), 1st Viscount Nelson, is revered as one of Britain's most heroic figures. The son of a Norfolk parson, Nelson rose through the ranks of the navy to become rear admiral before he turned forty. He lost his right arm fighting in the French Revolutionary Wars, won a decisive victory over the French at the Battle of the Nile in 1798, and in 1805 secured Britain's greatest naval victory at the Battle of Trafalgar. There he received a fatal gunshot wound. As he lay dying he is recorded as saying to Thomas Hardy, captain of his ship *HMS Victory*, 'Take care of poor Lady Hamilton,' (referring to Emma Hamilton, his infamous mistress) and, 'Kiss me, Hardy.' Nelson's Column in Trafalgar Square, London, was erected in his memory.

1807 The buying and selling of slaves is abolished in Britain and its empire, following anti-slavery campaigns by the Quakers in the 1700s and a protracted parliamentary campaign headed by politician and philanthropist William Wilberforce. In 1833, slavery is abolished in all of Britain's colonies.

1811 George III suffers a final relapse of mental illness, leading to his son George, Prince of Wales, becoming Prince Regent. Following his father's death in 1820, he is crowned George IV.

1815 Napoleon is finally defeated by the 1st Duke of Wellington, aided by the Prussians, at the Battle of Waterloo. According to Wellington, it was the 'nearest run thing you've ever seen in your life'. Wellington later served twice as prime minister for the Tory Party (January 1828 to November 1830, and November 1834 to December 1834). When Wellington died in 1852, he was given a state funeral like Nelson before him.

'I see no reason to suppose that these machines will ever force themselves into general use.'

THE DUKE OF WELLINGTON, IN REFERENCE TO STEAM LOCOMOTIVES, 1827.

1825 George Stephenson, having improved the design of the steam-powered train with his 'Rocket' steam train, opens the world's first passenger-train line between Stockton and Darlington, in north-east England.

1829   Catholic emancipation gives Catholics in Britain and Ireland the right to become MPs and take office.

1830   William IV, younger brother of George IV, becomes king.

1832   The Great Reform Act extends the vote to all male property owners, although the majority of working men (and all women) are still excluded. Over the following years, campaigners called the Chartists present petitions demanding an extension of the franchise. In 1867, the Second Reform Act gives the vote to all male householders in towns.

1837   Queen Victoria, William IV's niece, ascends the throne at the age of eighteen.

1845–51   The Irish potato famine, during which approximately 1 million people die and a further 1 million emigrate, many to North America and cities in England.

1846   The repeal of the Corn Laws makes Britain a free-trade nation.

1853–6   Britain with Turkey and France defeat Russia in the Crimean War. During the conflict, Queen Victoria introduces the Victoria Cross. Thousands of allied troops die from disease, although conditions improve with the intervention of the nurse and healthcare reformer Florence Nightingale.

QUEEN BEE

Reigning for sixty-three years, Queen Victoria (1819–1901) resided over a vast empire, whose territories included Canada, Australia, New Zealand and parts of Africa.

She married her beloved Prince Albert in 1840, with whom she had nine children. When he died in 1861, Victoria fell into a deep depression and wore black for the remainder of her reign. Her subsequent withdrawal from public life made her unpopular, but by the mid-1870s she re-emerged and her popularity was restored.

In 1876, she was made Empress of India and it was during her reign that the idea of a constitutional monarch, meaning one that remains above politics, was further entrenched. Following several acts to extend the right to vote, including the 1867 Second Reform Act, Victoria's political influence was reduced.

She came to symbolize the British Empire, and both her Golden (1887) and Diamond (1897) Jubilees were celebrated with much zeal. She died on 22 January 1901 and was buried at Windsor alongside her beloved husband.

1857–8   The Indian Mutiny (also known as the Indian Rebellion or the 1857 War of Independence) sees Indian soldiers in the Bengal army of the East India Company revolt against their British officers. Mutiny spreads to the civil population. The rebellion is crushed and the British Crown takes control of India, heralding the beginning of the Raj. A vast rail network is built and India becomes an even greater source of wealth and prestige for Britain.

1857   Women are granted the right to divorce. In 1882 women are also granted the right to keep assets and earnings when married.

'He speaks to me as if I was a public meeting.'

QUEEN VICTORIA OF GLADSTONE.

1868   The British Liberal statesman William Gladstone becomes prime minister, serving four times (1868–74, 1880–5, February to July 1886 and 1892–4). A passionately committed public statesman, Gladstone introduces many social reforms, including educational reforms that make school attendance compulsory for children up to the age of twelve. Gladstone also proposes Home Rule (self-government) in Ireland but is defeated in 1886 and 1893. He is famous for his poor relations with Queen Victoria and for his rivalry with Benjamin Disraeli (see page 60).

CLIMBING THE GREASY POLE

In 1874, Benjamin Disraeli became Tory prime minister (after a brief stint in February 1868 to December of the same year) and stayed in office until 1880. A brilliant statesman and speaker, he was largely responsible for increasing Britain's confidence in its imperial ambitions in gaining control of the Suez Canal, and for modernizing the Conservative Party.

'I never deny; I never contradict; I sometimes forget.'

WHEN TALKING TO QUEEN VICTORIA, WITH WHOM HE GOT ON FAMOUSLY, DISRAELI OBSERVED THIS SIMPLE RULE.

'There are three kinds of lies: lies, damned lies and statistics.'

ATTRIBUTED TO DISRAELI BY WRITER MARK TWAIN, THIS PHRASE IS OFTEN USED TO SHOW THAT STATISTICS ARE USED TO BOLSTER WEAK ARGUMENTS.

1880s Britain and other European nations conduct a series of military campaigns to seize land in Africa, known as the 'Scramble for Africa'. With large parts of Africa, all of India and Australia, the British Empire grows into the largest empire ever known, covering, at its peak, one-quarter of the word's land mass.

1880–1 and 1899–1902 The Boer Wars between Dutch settlers in South Africa and the British Empire. The British defeat the Dutch in the Second Boer War.

THE TWENTIETH CENTURY

'This is not a time for sound bites. We've left them at home. I feel the hand of history upon our shoulders ...'

PRIME MINISTER TONY BLAIR, 1998.

1901 Edward VII becomes king.

1903 Since the late nineteenth century, women's suffrage societies have been campaigning for better rights for women and the right to vote. In 1903, Emmeline Pankhurst forms the militant Women's Social and Political Union (WSPU), known as the Suffragettes. It wages a bitter and much-publicized campaign, including tactics such as arson attacks, to secure the vote for women.

1910 George V takes the throne.

1911 MPs are given a salary for the first time.

1914–18 The First World War (see page 62).

THE GREAT WAR

In June 1914, a teenage Bosnian Serb assassinated Archduke Franz Ferdinand, heir to the Austrian throne. A series of complex alliances, brought about by a build-up of tensions between the great powers of Europe, alongside increasing militarism and nationalism, led to the European powers being drawn into the conflict. Britain declared war on Germany on 4 August after Germany had invaded Belgium. The Allies comprised Great Britain, France, Russia, Japan, Belgium and Serbia, and later Italy, Portugal, Romania and the USA, while the Central Powers of Germany and Austria-Hungary were allied with the Ottoman Empire and Bulgaria. All of Britain's colonies were involved in the war, with more than 1 million Indians fighting, as well as thousands of Kenyans, West Indians, Canadians and Australians.

Soldiers faced poison gas and a barrage of lethal new weaponry and explosives (in the form of powerful artillery, machine-gun fire and hand grenades), often sat in trenches just a few metres away from the enemy. In July 1916, the British attack on the Somme led to one of the bloodiest battles ever recorded with over 1 million casualties (including 57,470 British casualties, 19,000 of them killed, on the first day alone). In September 1918, the Allies, with the help of the newly arrived American forces, pushed the German army from the Western Front. An armistice was signed at 11 a.m. on 11 November 1918. The war led to a total of 8.5 million deaths and a further 30 million civilian and military casualties.

1918   A flu pandemic, known as 'Spanish Flu', emerges, killing 200,000 in Britain and approximately 3 per cent of the world's population.

1918   Women over thirty are given the right to vote.

1921   Prime Minister Lloyd George negotiates the Anglo-Irish Treaty, which gives separate dominion status to Ireland as an 'Irish Free State', with the exception of six counties in Ulster that form Northern Ireland.

1924   The first Labour government is established under James Ramsay MacDonald.

1926   The General Strike is called by the TUC in support of the coal miners' demand for a wage increase. The 1929 Wall Street Crash and ensuing Great Depression leads Britain to suffer mass unemployment, particularly in the industrial and mining sectors.

1928   Women are granted equal voting rights with men.

1936   Edward VIII becomes king but abdicates months later to marry American divorcee Wallis Simpson (see below).

DECISION TIME

'When I was a little boy in Worcestershire reading history books, I never thought I should have to interfere between a king and his mistress.'

PRIME MINISTER STANLEY BALDWIN ON THE ABDICATION CRISIS.

King Edward VIII's intention to marry American Wallis Simpson caused a constitutional crisis in Britain as it was deemed unacceptable for the nominal head of the Church of England to marry someone who had married twice before. It fell to Prime Minister Stanley Baldwin to refuse permission for the marriage, telling the king he should renounce Simpson or abdicate. Edward chose the latter.

1936   Edward's brother George VI becomes king.

ROUND TWO

'In spite of the hardness and ruthlessness I thought I saw in his face, I got the impression that here was a man who could be relied upon when he had given his word.'

BRITISH PM NEVILLE CHAMBERLAIN ON HITLER, 19 SEPTEMBER 1938.

Desperate to avoid another conflict, Britain and France adopted a policy of appeasement towards the German chancellor, Adolf Hitler, (who by 1938 had reoccupied the Rhineland – revoking one of the terms of the Treaty of Versailles – annexed Austria and had begun the piecemeal occupation of Czechoslovakia). The Munich Agreement signed in September 1938, as a result of a private meeting between Hitler, the British PM, Mussolini and French PM Daladier, led to Chamberlain declaring on his return home that he had secured 'peace in our times'. Months later, however, Hitler disregarded the terms of the agreement, occupied Bohemia and Moravia in March 1939, and on 1 September launched a lightning attack on Poland, leaving Britain no other option but to declare war on Germany two days later. By the end of the war, there was strong public belief that Chamberlain had made serious diplomatic and military misjudgements and nearly caused Britain's defeat.

1939–45 The Second World War erupts, involving most of the world's nations, which ultimately form two opposing forces made up of the Allies, which initially consist of France, Poland and Great Britain, and later British Commonwealth countries, the USA, the Soviet Union and China, and the Axis powers, which include fascist Germany and Italy and the Empire of Japan. Over 50 million lives are lost as a result of the war, many of them civilian.

1940 In September, sustained bombing of British cities, known as the Blitz, breaks out and lasts until May 1941, killing some 40,000 civilians.

1942 Under General Montgomery, Allied forces secure a decisive victory over German and Italian forces at Al Alamein on the Egyptian coast. By May 1943, the Allies control the whole of the North African coast.

1942–5 Strategic US and British bombings of German cities and military zones result in 750,000 to 1 million civilian deaths.

1943 In July, Allied forces overthrow Mussolini and begin to conquer Italy. Meanwhile, in the Battle of the Atlantic, German U-boats attack Allied merchant shipping until better radar and intelligence gleaned through the British decryption of the German cipher machine, Enigma, enables Britain, from 1943, to reroute convoys away from German 'wolf packs'.

BRITISH BULLDOG

'I have nothing to offer but blood, toil, tears and sweat. We have before us an ordeal of the most grievous kind.'

ON BECOMING PM IN 1940.

Winston Churchill (1874–1965) twice served as Conservative prime minister (1940–5 and 1951–5) and when he died in 1965, Queen Elizabeth II granted him the honour of a state funeral.

After Neville Chamberlain's resignation in May 1940, Winston Churchill took up the helm and his tireless work, electrifying speeches and refusal to surrender to the Germans won over the British public and inspired the country during some of its darkest years. He was seen by many as the 'greatest statesman of the twentieth century' and was named the Greatest Briton of all time in a 2002 poll.

1944 On 6 June (known as D-Day), the Allied invasion of German-occupied France begins with Allied troops landing on five Normandy beaches. Thereafter, Allied troops break through German defences, liberate Paris, push through Europe and enter Germany in March 1945.

1944 Conservative Richard Butler oversees the Education Act, which introduces free secondary education in England and Wales.

1945 On 8 May, the Allies accept Germany's unconditional surrender and declare Victory in Europe.

'No one would go to Hitler's funeral if he was alive today.'

LABOUR MP RON BROWN, 1989.

1945 Fifty member nations, including Britain, sign the United Nations Charter.

1947 India is granted independence from Britain and divides into two new states: India and the Muslim state of Pakistan.

1948 The National Health Service, offering free health care for everyone, is introduced under Clement Attlee's Labour government.

1948 People from Ireland and the West Indies are invited to migrate to the UK. The ship *Empire Windrush* arrives, bringing 500 Jamaican immigrants to Britain.

A FAIRER SOCIETY

Labour's landslide victory in 1945 resulted in Clement Attlee (1883–1967) becoming PM. In 1948, he and his cabinet, including his minister of health, Aneurin 'Nye' Bevan, brought in laws to create a 'Welfare State' in a bid to remove the 'evil giants' of British society (as outlined by the economist Sir William Beveridge in 1942). His national system of benefits was designed to protect people 'from cradle to grave'. He also nationalized large industries, like coal mining, steel and electricity and the rail network.

1949 Ten European states set up the Council of Europe via the Treaty of London to promote co-operation, human rights and democracy.

1952 Elizabeth II becomes queen.

1954 Rationing ends and the British begin to prosper, with many able to afford new gadgets such as washing machines and televisions. This change prompts Conservative PM Harold Macmillan to declare in 1959, 'Most of our people have never had it so good.'

1956 Egypt takes control of the British and French-owned Suez canal, leading to the Suez Crisis.

1961 The first contraceptive pill goes on sale. The increased use of the pill in the 1960s and 70s allows women to limit the number of children they have and plan their families.

1963 The Profumo Affair erupts (see below).

A MESSY AFFAIR

'A great party is not to be brought down because of a squalid affair between a woman of easy virtue and a proved liar.'

CONSERVATIVE POLITICIAN LORD HAILSHAM.

The sexual scandal known as the Profumo Affair arose after it was discovered that John Profumo, Secretary of State for War, had had an affair with Christine Keeler, the reputed mistress of a Soviet spy. His subsequent denial of the affair in the House of Commons led to his resignation in 1963 and damaged the reputation of Harold Macmillan's Conservative government. Macmillan resigned a few months later due to ill health (thought to have been exacerbated by the scandal) and the Conservatives lost the general election the following year.

1965 Death penalty abolished.

1966   England wins the football World Cup.

1969   The voting age is changed to eighteen.

1972   On 30 January, British soldiers shoot dead thirteen unarmed men and injure fourteen in Derry, Northern Ireland, subsequently known as Bloody Sunday. In March, further unrest leads to the suspension of the Northern Ireland Parliament.

1973   Britain joins the European Economic Community (EEC).

1974   A combination of slow growth of the economy in the 1960s and 1970s, the 1973 oil crisis and strike action by trade unions leads to the government enforcing the three-day working week from 1 January to 7 March 1974 in a bid to conserve electricity.

1979   Margaret Thatcher becomes Conservative PM.

> 'It is exciting to have a real crisis on your hands, when you have spent half your political life dealing with humdrum issues like the environment.'
>
> MARGARET THATCHER, ON THE FALKLANDS CAMPAIGN, 1982.

1982 In April, the Falklands War breaks out following an Argentine invasion. Margaret Thatcher immediately despatches a naval task force, which retakes the islands. The Argentines surrender in June.

THE IRON LADY

Born in 1925, in Grantham, Lincolnshire, the daughter of a grocer, Margaret Thatcher is the only woman to have held the office of prime minister and is the longest-serving PM of the twentieth century. Having studied at Somerville, Oxford, she first worked as a research chemist and later qualified as a barrister. Involved in local Conservative party politics, she fought unsuccessfully as the prospective Conservative candidate in the general elections of the early 1950s, finally being elected to the safe seat of Finchley in 1959.

In 1951 she married businessman Denis Thatcher and two years later gave birth to twins Mark and Carol. In 1964 she was promoted to the shadow cabinet and in 1970, under Conservative PM Ted Heath, she took the post of Education Secretary, during which time she implemented the withdrawal of milk for seven to eleven-year-olds, leading the press to dub her 'Margaret Thatcher, Milk Snatcher'. In 1975, she defeated Heath in a party leadership election and became Leader of the Opposition. In 1976, the Russian government nicknamed her the 'Iron Lady' for her staunch opposition to socialism.

Following a series of strikes during the winter of 1978–9 (known as the Winter of Discontent), Thatcher became PM. She cut inflation and introduced bills to curb union militancy, privatize state industry, boost the free market and run down old-style manufacturing, with the result that unemployment ran above 3 million.

In 1983, after victory in the Falklands, she won a landslide victory, defeated the UK miners' strike in 1985, and won a third term of office in 1987. Poll tax riots and her antipathy towards the European Union led to dissatisfaction within the Conservatives, and a leadership challenge caused her to resign in 1990.

Given a life peerage in 1992, she suffered a series of small strokes in 2002 and died in 2013 after a final stroke at the age of eighty-seven. On 17 April 2013, she received a ceremonial funeral, with full military honours, at St Paul's Cathedral.

1984–5 The UK miners' strike is defeated and the British trade union movement is significantly weakened.

1989 The Cold War ends with the fall of the Berlin Wall and the collapse of the Soviet Union two years later.

1990–1 The Gulf War. Britain plays a key role in the Coalition Force, following the invasion of Kuwait by Iraq. The war leads to the liberation of Kuwait and advances into Iraqi territory.

1990 John Major becomes Conservative prime minister.

1992 British forces form part of the peacekeeping UN forces in Croatia and later Bosnia.

1994 The Channel Tunnel opens, linking Britain to France (see page 97). The EEC becomes the European Union.

1997 In May, Tony Blair, leader of the Labour Party, wins a landslide victory in the general election and becomes prime minister. His brand of 'New Labour' seeks to distance itself from traditional socialism.

1997 In August, Diana, Princess of Wales, dies in a car crash, leading to an outpouring of grief around the country. Blair remembers her as the 'People's Princess'.

1998 The Good Friday Agreement gives hope for peace in Northern Ireland.

1999 The UK takes a lead role in NATO forces against Slobodan Milošević's forces in Kosovo.

1999 The Welsh Assembly and Scottish Parliament are both established. The Northern Ireland Assembly is elected but suspended in 2002, then reinstated in 2007.

2001   As part of a global war on international terrorism, the UK joins other NATO forces led by the US in invading Taliban-ruled Afghanistan. Britain operates in Afghanistan as part of the United Nations' International Security Assistant Force (ISAF) until the end of 2014, when the last British forces leave Helmand.

2003   British forces take part in the invasion of Iraq, ending combat operations in 2009.

2004   In October, Tony Blair announces he will seek a third term in office but not a fourth. Nevertheless, his party wins again in May 2005 and it isn't until September 2006 that Blair announces he will step down within the year.

2007   Gordon Brown, Blair's Chancellor of the Exchequer – and the man with whom he holds an alleged gentleman's agreement that states he will one day pass on the baton of leadership – becomes Labour prime minister.

2008   The ongoing global financial crisis leads to the British government offering a bailout package to UK banks, totalling £500 billion.

2010   After a hung parliament, the Conservative and Liberal Democrat parties form a coalition government, with Conservative Party leader David Cameron as prime minister and Liberal Democrat Party leader Nick Clegg deputy prime minister.

AWKWARD

During the May 2010 electoral campaign, when asked by a reporter for his favourite political joke, David Cameron answered, 'Nick Clegg, at the moment.' Cameron looked awkward when he was reminded of this at his first news conference with Nick Clegg following the formation of the coalition government.

2012   The Queen's Diamond Jubilee is celebrated with a pageant of 1,000 boats on the River Thames, the burning of 2,012 beacons across the UK and Commonwealth, and a BBC concert at Buckingham Palace.

2012   In the summer months, London hosts the 2012 Olympic and Paralympic Games. It is seen by many as a national triumph, generating huge public enthusiasm and widespread acclaim for the thousands of volunteers and the head of the Olympic Committee, Sebastian Coe, for their organization of the proceedings.

2015   The Conservatives win the general election with a majority, thus ending the coalition government, and David Cameron remains prime minister.

GREAT BRITONS

The great and the good of the UK's history unite in a section that celebrates notable characters of the past.

BANKNOTES

'It makes me look so old. But then I suppose I am old.'
QUEEN ELIZABETH, ON THE NEWLY DESIGNED £5 NOTES, JUNE 1990.

The banknotes of the United Kingdom are denominated in pounds sterling (GBP; 'sterling' probably derives from Old English *steorra*, star, because early Norman pennies bore that emblem). The most common slang term for the British pound is 'quid' (derived probably from the Latin phrase *quid pro quo*, 'something for something', in relation to the trade of money for goods). Queen Elizabeth II's portrait has featured on all Treasury notes since 1960, and she is one of only two British monarchs ever to have been depicted on a UK – as distinct from a Scottish – banknote. Leading British figures have also featured on banknotes since 1970. These are:

The current £5 note features Elizabeth Fry (1780–1845), an English Quaker and prison and social reformer, who was a major driving force behind new legislation to make treatment of prisoners more humane. The main illustration shows Fry reading to prisoners at London's infamous Newgate Prison. In 2013, the Bank of England governor announced that from 2016 Sir Winston Churchill will replace Elizabeth Fry, who is the only woman other than the Queen currently to be represented on a British banknote.

The current £10 note features Charles Darwin (1809–82), the Victorian naturalist who developed the theory of evolution. Also pictured is an illustration of Darwin's own magnifying lens and some of the flora and fauna that he encountered on his travels, as well as the ship HMS *Beagle*, in which he made his most famous voyage.

In 2016, Darwin will be replaced by a portrait of author Jane Austen (1775–1817) and an illustration of her writing table, along with a quote from *Pride and Prejudice*.

The £10 note featuring the great Victorian novelist and social critic Charles Dickens (1812–70) was withdrawn in 2003.

The current £20 note depicts the Scottish economist Adam Smith (1723–90). He produced the first defence of free-market economics, *An Enquiry into the Nature and Causes of the Wealth of Nations*, and is regarded as the father of modern economics, and one of the founders of capitalism.

The £20 note featuring the English composer Sir Edward Elgar (1857–1934), whose orchestral works included the *Pomp and Circumstance* marches, was withdrawn in June 2010.

The current £50 note features Sir John Houblon (1632–1712), the first governor of the Bank of England. The note also shows his house on Threadneedle Street, the site of the present Bank of England building.

Introduced in November 2011, a more recent £50 note features the English manufacturer Matthew Boulton (1728–1809) and the Scottish engineer James Watt (1736–1819). The pair produced and sold the Boulton & Watt steam engine, which contributed significantly to the mechanization of factories and mills in the late eighteenth century.

Northern Ireland and Scotland also have their own banknotes, which are valid across the UK, although businesses and shops do not have to accept them.

The Bank of Scotland notes (£100, £50, £20, £10 and £5) feature the Scottish novelist, playwright and poet Sir Walter Scott (1771–1832). He achieved international fame during his own lifetime and his classic work includes the novel *Ivanhoe* and the popular poem 'The Lady of the Lake'. His portrait is considered worthy of appearance because he's credited with being the saviour of the Scottish banknote, having campaigned in the 1820s to stop Parliament forcing Scottish banks to discontinue producing Scottish pound notes.

In Northern Ireland, four banks are licensed to issue notes and each bank has its own design. Bank of Ireland notes (£20, £10 and £5) feature an illustration of the Old Bushmills (whisky) Distillery, and other bank notes include a generic couple on one side with images commemorating the Armada shipwreck off the coast of County Antrim on the other, a US space shuttle, and other figures including J. B. Dunlop (Scotsman and founder of the Dunlop Rubber Company who moved to Belfast).

GREAT BRITISH INVENTORS

Isaac Newton (1643–1727) English physicist and mathematician and the most influential scientist of his era. He built the first practical reflecting telescope, investigated the refraction of light, and his greatest work, *Principia Mathematica*, formulated the laws of motion and showed how the universal force gravity affects all parts of the universe (including the orbit of the planets).

Abraham Darby (1678–1717) In 1709, Quaker Abraham Darby developed a method of producing pig iron from coke, which advanced the mass production of brass and iron goods. It also facilitated the Industrial Revolution, because up until this point most industrial machines, such as steam engines and the railway, had been made from iron.

James Watt (1736–1819) Scottish engineer James Watt improved and developed the steam engine so that it could run factory machines. By 1800, Watt's engine became the mechanical workhorse of the Industrial Revolution, powering some 500 of Britain's mines, mills and factories. The SI unit of power, the watt, is named after him.

George Stephenson (1781–1848) Known as the 'Father of Railways', English engineer George Stephenson opened the first passenger steam-powered train between

Liverpool and Manchester in 1830. His 'Rocket' steam engine improved the design of the first steam-powered train produced by Richard Trevithick in 1803, and by 1855 thousands of miles of railway tracks crossed Britain.

Isambard Kingdom Brunel (1806–59) Revolutionized engineering and transport, constructing 125 bridges, over 1,000 miles of railway, numerous tunnels and three steamships, including the SS *Great Western*, the first steamship to make regular trans-Atlantic crossings between Bristol and New York.

Charles Darwin (1809–82) Scientist and naturalist Charles Darwin published *On the Origin of Species by Means of Natural Selection* in 1859, which detailed his theory of evolution by natural selection. Destroying the prevailing orthodoxy on how the world was created, his theory has become one of the most influential scientific ideas ever conceived.

Joseph Swan (1828–1914) In 1878, British physicist Joseph Swan invented and demonstrated the electric light bulb (prior to, and independently of, American inventor Thomas Edison, who later secured the American patent for the light bulb). The Houses of Parliament and the British Museum were two of the first public buildings to be lit by electricity.

Alexander Graham Bell (1847–1922) In 1876, the Scottish-born and appropriately named Bell was largely credited with inventing the telephone in the US by using telegraph technology to transmit the sound of voices.

Alexander Fleming (1881–1955) A Scottish biologist who, when investigating the properties of staphylococcus bacteria, discovered mould growing on one of his cultures, which he identified as being from the Penicillium genus. His discovery ultimately led to the use of antibiotics and changed modern medicine.

John Logie Baird (1888–1946) In 1926, Scotsman Baird gave the world's first demonstration of a television before fifty scientists in a London attic. In 1927 he made the first television broadcast between London and Scotland.

Sir Robert Watson-Watt (1892–1973) A descendant of James Watt, Robert Watson-Watt developed the use of radar, having proposed to the War Ministry in 1935 that it could be used to detect enemy aircraft. Radar played an invaluable role in the Allies' victory in the Second World War.

Alan Turing (1912–54) British mathematician Turing (and later wartime code-breaker) developed a theoretical mathematical device, known as the Turing machine, which was influential in computational theory and the development of modern computers.

Frank Whittle (1907–96) In the 1930s, this English RAF engineer officer developed the turbojet engine.

Francis Crick (1916–2004) English molecular biologist who co-discovered (along with J. D. Watson) the structure of DNA molecules in 1953. He played a crucial role in research leading to the genetic code.

Sir Tim Berners-Lee (1955–) Invented the World Wide Web, based on a concept of hypertext that would allow researchers to share information anywhere. The world's first website was launched in 1991.

'THIS SCEPTRED ISLE':
GEOGRAPHY

'We are not wholly an island, except geographically.'

FORMER PM JOHN MAJOR ON BRITAIN'S RELATIONSHIP
WITH EUROPE, 1992.

Britain is a small and fairly compact country, the third most-populated island in the world and twice as densely populated as France.

Great Britain covers 93,851 sq miles (243,073 sq km), of which England makes up two-thirds at 50,302 sq miles (130,281 sq km); Wales covers 8,005 sq miles (20,732 sq km) and Scotland 30,087 sq miles (77,925 sq km), with Northern Ireland at 5,457 sq miles (14,135 sq km).

The longest distance on the island of Great Britain is from Land's End in Cornwall to John O'Groats in Caithness, Scotland, at approximately 870 miles (1,400 km) by road. The English east coast and the Welsh west coast are 300 miles (483 km) apart.

AN ISLAND MENTALITY

Great Britain's island status has had considerable impact on the mentality of the British. The surrounding sea has not only engendered a feeling of isolation from Europe, manifest in the British distrust of its continental neighbours, but it has also crucially provided protection from its invading armies. Unlike most other European nations, Britain has never needed a vast standing army; instead, particularly from the late seventeenth century, Britain focused on building its naval fleet, so that by the late eighteenth century, Britain, as the world's leading maritime power, could accumulate a vast colonial empire. As Winston Churchill put it to the House of Commons on 13 May 1901: 'We in this fortunate, happy island, relieved by our insular position of a double burden, may turn our individual efforts and attention to the Fleet.'

POPULATION

At the last census of 2011, the population of the UK was 63.2 million (31 million men and 32.2 million women). England housed 53 million, Scotland 5.3 million, Wales 3.1 million and Northern Ireland 1.8 million people respectively.

The population density of the UK is one of the highest in the world, with almost one-third of the country's inhabitants living in the south-east of England, just over 8 million of whom live in London.

Between 2001 and 2011, the British population increased by 4.1 million, with England and Wales seeing the largest growth since the census was first taken in 1801. The highest population growth was in London, which gained 850,000 residents; the south-east also saw large growth, gaining some 611,000 residents. The lowest increase was in the north-east, which gained 56,600 residents in the same period.

People are also living for longer in the UK, with 10.4 million people (one in six) aged sixty-five and over. In 2011, 430,000 UK residents were aged ninety and over, compared with 340,000 in 2001 and just 13,000 in 1911.

According to the Office of National Statistics, around one-third of babies born in the United Kingdom are expected to survive their 100th birthday. As of 2011, female life expectancy at birth is 82.1 years and male life expectancy 78.1 years.

CITIES

There are sixty-nine official cities in the United Kingdom (fifty-one in England, seven in Scotland, six in Wales and five in Northern Ireland). City status is granted by the Crown and, in England and Wales, was traditionally given to towns with diocesan cathedrals, as established by King Henry VIII in the 1540s. However, since 1888, the existence of a cathedral is no longer a relevant factor in the granting of city status (other considerations, such as population, are taken into account).

London (known in local government as Greater London), the capital of the United Kingdom, does not have official city status as it already comprises the City of London and the Westminster London Borough (or City of Westminster), along with another thirty-one London boroughs. It is the largest city in Europe, with a population in 2011 of approximately 8,174,000, covering 625 sq miles (1,600 sq km).

'Leeds is the biggest city of its size in Europe.'
GREG MULHOLLAND, LIBERAL DEMOCRAT MEMBER FOR LEEDS, 2005.

Leeds in West Yorkshire is the third-biggest city in England with a population in 2011 of approximately 750,700. Outside London, only Birmingham in the West Midlands is more populous than Leeds, with a population in 2011 of 1,073,000 (an increase of 96,000 since 2001).

Cities in the UK which have 500,000 residents or more are: London, Birmingham, Glasgow, Leeds, Bradford, Sheffield, Liverpool, Manchester, Belfast, Bristol, Newcastle-upon-Tyne and Nottingham.

RIVERS

The longest river in the UK is the River Severn at 220 miles (354 km) in length. It rises in the Cambrian Mountains in Powys, mid-Wales, then flows through Shropshire, Worcestershire and Gloucestershire, and flows as the Severn Estuary out into the Bristol Channel and the Atlantic Ocean.

The River Severn (England and Wales): 220 miles (354 km).

The River Thames (London and Oxford): 215 miles (346 km).

The River Trent (the Midlands): 185 miles (297 km).

The River Great Ouse (East Anglia): 143 miles (230 km).

The River Wye (Wales and England): 135 miles (215 km).

The River Tay (east Scotland): 117 miles (188 km).

The River Spey (north-east Scotland): 107 miles (172 km).

The River Clyde (south-west Scotland): 106 miles (172 km).

The River Tweed (Scottish borders): 96 miles (155 km).

The River Nene (Northamptonshire and east England): 91 miles (147 km).

THE TEN LONGEST RIVERS IN THE UK

GET BEHIND THE BARRIER

The Thames Barrier is one of the world's largest movable flood barriers (second only to the Eastern Scheldt storm-surge barrier in the Netherlands). Designed by Charles Draper, it became operational in 1982 and has ten steel gates that can be raised into position. Spanning 520 metres (570 yards) near Woolwich, the barrier protects central London from flooding caused by tidal surges. As of April 2015, the Barrier has been closed 175 times to protect London from flooding. In 1953, a major flood on the east coast of England and the Thames Estuary caused 300 deaths, highlighting the need for flood defences for London.

MODEL VILLAGE

The village of New Lanark, which comprised cotton mills and housing for its workers, was built on the banks of the River Clyde, South Lanarkshire, in 1786 by industrialist David Dale and social reformer Robert Owen. Water was drawn from the river to power the mill machinery. The amenities and housing for the workers were excellent and the mills thrived commercially – a venture celebrated throughout Europe as the epitome of utopian socialism.

DISTRICTS AND REGIONS OF THE UK

Northern Ireland is made up of six counties: County Antrim, County Armagh, County Down, County Fermanagh, County Londonderry, County Tyrone. (Although local government no longer recognizes these counties, instead dividing Northern Ireland into twenty-six districts.) These six counties were originally in the historic province of Ulster, and Northern Ireland is often referred to as Ulster despite three of the original Ulster counties – Canan, Donegal and Monaghan – forming part of the Republic of Ireland.

DIALECT

The United Kingdom has distinct regional identities, each reflected in its varied language and culture, as well as the UK's many different dialects and accents.

Welsh, an ancient Celtic language, is spoken by about 19 per cent of the Welsh population, according to the 2011 census, and is taught in schools (compulsorily up to the age of sixteen for state school pupils) and universities.

Scottish Gaelic, as its name suggests, is a Celtic language native to Scotland, although, according to the 2011 census, only around 1.2 per cent of Scots speak it (largely in the Highlands and on the islands).

Irish or Irish Gaelic (from which Scottish Gaelic is derived) is spoken in Northern Ireland. According to the 2011 census, around 11 per cent of the population of Northern Ireland have some knowledge of Irish. Most Irish speakers in Ulster speak the Donegal dialect of Ulster Irish.

Other well-known dialects in England are:

Scouse (Liverpool) 'Scouse' comes from 'lobscouse', the name for a meat stew formerly eaten by sailors and which became popular in Liverpool. People who ate the stew were known as 'scousers'.

Geordie (Tyneside) There are lots of theories behind the derivation of the word Geordie, one being that it's a familiar form of 'George', a very common name for coalmen in the north-east of England. Famously incomprehensible to foreigners (and other Brits), Geordie boasts an array of common words, including: alreet (alright), bairn (child), howay (hurry up, come on), nowt (nothing), ma (mother), nooadays (these days), y'kin (you can), canny (pleasant), guzzling (eating).

Brummie (Birmingham) The word derives from Bromwicham or Brummagem, the historical variant to the name Birmingham.

Cockney (London) Chaucer used the word 'cokenay' to describe a pampered child and by the sixteenth century it was used as a derogatory reference for effeminate town-dwellers. By the following century, the word was defined to apply only to those born in the City of London within the sound of the Bow Bells (i.e. the bells of St Mary-le-Bow in the City).

DISTRICTS AND REGIONS OF THE UK

Orkney Islands

Channel Islands

Scotland

1 Highland
2 Moray
3 Aberdeenshire
4 Angus
5 Perth and Kinross
6 Argyll and Bute
7 Stirling
8 Clackmannanshire
9 Fife
10 Dunbartonshire
11 Helensburgh and Lomond
12 North Lanarkshire
13 Falkirk
14 West Lothian
15 Edinburgh
16 East Lothian
17 Midlothian
18 Inverclyde
19 Renfrewshire
20 Glasgow
21 North Ayrshire
22 East Renfrewshire
23 East Ayrshire
24 South Lanarkshire
25 Scottish Borders
26 South Ayrshire
27 Dumfries and Galloway

England

28 Northumberland
29 Cumbria
30 Durham
31 North Yorkshire
32 Isle of Man
33 Lancashire
34 West Yorkshire
35 East Yorkshire
36 Merseyside
37 Greater Manchester
38 South Yorkshire
39 Cheshire
40 Derbyshire
41 Nottinghamshire
42 Lincolnshire
43 Shropshire
44 Staffordshire
45 Leicestershire
46 Rutland
47 Norfolk
48 West Midlands
49 Herefordshire
50 Worcestershire
51 Warwickshire
52 Northamptonshire
53 Huntingdonshire

England (continued)

54 Cambridgeshire
55 Suffolk
56 Gloucestershire
57 Oxfordshire
58 Buckinghamshire
59 Bedfordshire
60 Hertfordshire
61 Essex
62 Wiltshire
63 Berkshire
64 Greater London
65 Cornwall
66 Devon
67 Somerset
68 Dorset
69 Hampshire
70 Isle of Wight
71 Surrey
72 West Sussex
73 East Sussex
74 Kent

Wales

75 Anglesey
76 Gwynedd
77 Conwy
78 Denbighshire
79 Flintshire
80 Wrexham
81 Ceredigion
82 Powys
83 Pembrokeshire
84 Carmarthenshire
85 Swansea and the Gower
86 Neath
87 Bridgend
88 Rhondda Cynon Taff
89 Merthyr Tydfil
90 Glamorgan
91 Cardiff
92 Caerphilly
93 Blaenau Gwent
94 Monmouthshire
95 Torfaen
96 Newport

Northern Ireland

A Fermanagh
B Tyrone
C Londonderry
D Antrim
E Down
F Armagh

NATIONAL PARKS

National parks are areas of scenic landscape that are relatively undeveloped, as designated under the National Parks and Access to the Countryside Act 1949. There are fifteen national parks in England, Wales and Scotland, including the Peak District, which lies mainly in northern Derbyshire and the Lake District, Cumbria, which is the most visited national park in the United Kingdom, attracting 15.8 million visitors annually.

MOUNTAINS

The ten highest mountains in the UK are all in Scotland. The UK's highest mountain is Ben Nevis, located in the Grampian Mountains in the Scottish Highlands, which stands at 1,344 metres (4,409 feet) above sea level.

The highest mountain in Wales is Snowdon in Gwynedd, north Wales, which stands at 1,085 metres (3,560 feet) above sea level.

The highest mountain in England is Scafell Pike in the Lake District, which stands at 978 metres (3,209 feet) above sea level.

The highest mountain in Northern Ireland is Slieve Donard in County Down, which stands at 850 metres (2,789 feet) above sea level.

THE CHANNEL TUNNEL

For the first time since the Ice Age, Britain and France were linked with the opening of the Channel Tunnel (or 'Chunnel') in 1994. There are, in fact, three tunnels: two for rail traffic and a central tunnel for services and security. Each tunnel is 31 miles (50 km) long, 23 miles (37 km) of which is underwater, making it the longest undersea tunnel system in the world. The tunnels emerge at Folkestone in England and Sangatte near Calais in France, and passengers can travel either on trains or within their own cars, which are then loaded onto special rail cars.

A privately financed scheme (after the then prime minister Margaret Thatcher in 1986 insisted that 'not a public penny' should be sunk into the tunnel), the estimated cost of making the tunnel was £4.9 billion. This was a gross miscalculation, because by the time the tunnel opened in 1994, the cost had more than doubled to £12 billion. Over the years it has met a lot of controversy, not least the relative inadequacies of the British rail network on which Eurostar trains are forced to travel far more slowly than the speeds of 186 mph (299 kph) that they reach on French rails. Furthermore, in the late nineties, illegal immigrants were entering the UK via the tunnel; in 1996 a fire destroyed a Eurotunnel freight shuttle injuring thirty-four people; in 2009 five trains broke down, leaving 2,000 passengers stranded for several hours without food or water.

Despite these failures, the Channel Tunnel remains popular – in 2014 almost 21 million people and approximately 18.7 million tonnes of freight used it, and Eurostar passengers totalled 10.4 million in the same year.

BEEN HERE BEFORE

As early as 1802, the French engineer Albert Mathieu put forward a proposal for a tunnel to run under the Channel for horse-drawn carriages. In 1881, the British and French conducted exploratory work in tunnel digging before the project was abandoned in 1882, owing to concern made by politicians and newspapers that the tunnel would compromise Britain's natural defences.

BRITAIN'S RELATIONSHIP WITH FRANCE

'I liken the French/British relationship to a very old married couple who often think of killing each other but would never dream of divorce.'

FORMER LABOUR POLITICIAN DENIS MACSHANE, 15 JANUARY 2007.

Current relations between the UK and France are cordial, but there has always been an edge of wariness on both sides due to centuries of hostility (see pages 32–76). Britain's island status has partly contributed to a fear of its continental neighbours (France being the nearest) and despite the *Entente Cordial* (a 100-year alliance during which the two nations fought alongside each other in the First and Second World Wars) mutual disdain has never been far from the surface.

The French are known to the British as 'frogs' and any sexual or risqué behaviour is often qualified as 'French' (a kiss using tongues is known as a 'French kiss', a condom a 'French Letter', although interestingly, in France, spanking is known as 'le vice Anglais'), and former Conservative PM John Major was still using 'Excuse my French' (a phrase used to apologize for swearing) in the 1990s.

When asked by a French hotel receptionist to spell his name, Labour MP and journalist Woodrow Wyatt (1918–97) answered, 'Waterloo, Ypres, Agincourt, Trafalgar, Trafalgar'.

Despite this underlying scorn of the French, France is the go-to destination for millions of British holidaymakers as well as those seeking the ideal retirement location. Attracted by France's warmer climate, cuisine and relaxed pace of life, around 9 million English tourists head to France every year.

MIGRATION TO THE UK

Britain has often experienced large waves of migration to its shores, as well as periods of high emigration, which has largely kept its population in balance. During the 1970s and 1980s Britain's population experienced a net loss due to people emigrating to countries like Australia, New Zealand and Canada. Since the late 1990s, however, this trend has reversed with more migrants – many coming from central and Eastern Europe, as a result of the expansion of the European Union in 2004 – entering the country than leaving it. A large proportion of newcomers to Britain have traditionally come from India, Pakistan and Africa.

According to a report by the Office for National Statistics on the UK population in 2011, the most common non-UK country of birth is India (729,000) and the most common non-British nationality in the UK is Polish (687,000).

In 2011, the number of UK residents born abroad stood at 7.5 million (5.0 million from outside EU and 2.5 million from within the EU), representing 12 per cent of the UK population and an increase of 2.3 million since 2004.

The five most common countries of birth in the UK calendar years 2007–11 were (in order): India, Poland, Pakistan, Republic of Ireland and Germany. The five most common nationalities are Polish, Irish, Indian, Pakistani and American.

HOME FROM HOME

Britain has a tradition of offering safety to people fleeing persecution and hardship from abroad. In the sixteenth and eighteenth centuries, Huguenots (French Protestants) escaping persecution settled in the UK, as did the Irish during the Irish famine of the 1840s and Jewish people fleeing racist pogroms in Russia between 1880 and 1910.

In the late 1940s, increasing numbers of people from the Commonwealth countries of India, Pakistan and the West Indies came to the UK, often at the invitation of the British government, which needed workers to fill the manual and lower-paid jobs of an expanding economy. Immigration was further encouraged in the 1950s due to a shortage of labour in the UK. Many West Indians arrived to work in public transport, catering and the NHS, and Indians and Pakistanis worked for textile and engineering firms in the north and the Midlands.

In the 1960s and early 1970s, the government moved away from its open-door policy for Commonwealth immigrants by passing new laws that restricted the number of Commonwealth migrants coming into the UK. These required applicants to apply for a work voucher or permit, graded according to employment prospects. By 1972, only holders of work permits or people with one parent or one grandparent born in the UK could gain entry. During this time, however, the UK government still helped a large number of refugees to settle in the country, to include 27,000 Asians from Uganda and from the late 1970s, 25,000 refugees from South-East Asia.

NATIONALITY ACTS AND CITIZENSHIP

In 1981, new conditions for British nationality and redefinitions for British citizenship were passed stipulating that acceptance for settlement in the UK did not mean automatic British citizenship. More specific requirements were made in 2002 – anyone seeking British citizenship was required to sit a test to demonstrate their knowledge of life in Britain. They were also required to attend a citizenship ceremony and swear a citizenship oath and pledge to queen and country, and reach sufficient proficiency in the English language. This requirement was extended also to include people seeking to settle permanently in Britain.

The Life in the United Kingdom Test consists of twenty-four multiple-choice questions, covering topics such as history, society, government and the law. Candidates must answer at least eighteen questions correctly (75 per cent and above). On average, just under 71 per cent of applicants pass.

In 2007, Red Squirrel Publishing conducted a survey, testing over 15,000 Facebook users with a sample version of the citizenship exam. A sample test taken by 11,118 British people resulted in just 1,585 (14 per cent) achieving a pass score. In 2012, every member of the *New Statesman* magazine editorial team failed the test.

'YOUR MARRIAGE COMES BY DESTINY': SOCIETY

The changing nature of the family and threatened alterations to the education system means British society is always on the move.

FAMILIES, HOUSEHOLDS AND MARRIAGE

New social structures are emerging in the UK, with the traditional nuclear family (two married parents and two children) on the decrease. Households are getting smaller – the average size of a household in 2009 was just 2.4 people.

In 2011, there were 17.9 million families living in the UK, 12 million of which comprised married couples. Families made up of opposite-sex non-married couples increased from 2.1 million in 2001 to 2.9 million in 2011 (with the number of dependent children living with opposite-sex cohabiting couples increasing from 1.3 million to 1.8 million).

WITH THIS RING

Marriage law in the UK dictates that:

- Both members of the couple must be aged sixteen or over. If under eighteen they must have their parents' consent to marry (although no parental consent is needed in Scotland).

- No one can be forced to marry against their wishes.

- Prospective partners must not be already married or too closely related (although first cousins can still legally wed in the UK).

- At least two witnesses must sign the register on the day of the wedding.

A marriage can take place in, among other locations, a registered place of worship, a registered office or premises approved by the local authority.

There is a significant increase of adults living alone: in 2011, 7.7 million people lived alone, 2.5 million of whom came from the 45–64 age group (a sharp increase from around 1.7 million in 2001). This is due to several reasons: an increasing population in that age range, a decrease in married couples and a rise in divorce rates.

Families made up of same-sex cohabiting couples are on the increase, rising from 45,000 in 2001 to 63,000 in 2011. The number of civil-partner families in 2011 was 59,000.

Less than one-third of marriages are celebrated with a religious ceremony, and two in five marriages are remarriages by one or both of the parties concerned. Marriage is also happening at a much later age, with people increasingly seeing their twenties as the decade for education and career, leaving marriage and establishing a family to their thirties.

In 1981, the average age for women to marry was 23.1. By 2009 this had risen to 30. For men, it rose from an average age of 25.4 to 32.1 years within this same period.

ALL FOR ONE

In 2004, same-sex couples were entitled to form civil partnerships, which grants them most of the same rights as married couples. The end of 2011 saw a total of 53,417 civil partnerships formed since legislation came into force, far exceeding the estimates of the 2004 Labour government that between 11,000 and 22,000 people would enter partnerships by 2010. Initially, far more men entered into civil partnerships than women, although since 2007 the numbers have been balancing out. One-quarter of all civil partnerships take place in London, with the next most popular location being Brighton and Hove.

Since the introduction of the Marriage Act in 2013, same-sex couples are able to marry in England and Wales, with Scotland following in 2014. Religious organizations are able to opt in to perform these weddings and couples may also convert their civil partnership into a marriage if they wish.

SCANDAL

'It is time to get back to basics.'

FORMER CONSERVATIVE PM JOHN MAJOR IN A SPEECH AT THE
CONSERVATIVE PARTY CONFERENCE, 8 OCTOBER 1993.

Major's 'Back to Basics' campaign was intended to focus on law and order, education and social responsibilities, but it was interpreted by many as a moral campaign to promote traditional family values. It ultimately became associated with a string of 'sleaze' scandals involving Conservative MPs and cabinet ministers (including David Mellor, who had been exposed in 1992 for having had an affair with actress Antonia de Sancha). In September 2002, it was revealed that Major himself had had a four-year affair with fellow Tory MP Edwina Currie while serving as a backbencher. The media was quick to throw charges of hypocrisy in reference to his 'Back to Basics' campaign: 'MPs can't be expected to lead blameless lives. They are human. But the one sin they need never be guilty of is hypocrisy – telling us how to lead our lives while doing the opposite themselves.' The *Mirror*, as quoted in *The Guardian*, Monday 30 September 2002.

Major subsequently issued a statement on the affair, saying, 'It is the one event in my life of which I am most ashamed and I have long feared that would be made public.' His former paramour responded by saying, '… he may say now he's ashamed of it but he wasn't ashamed of it at the time and he wanted it to go on.'

DIVORCE

Divorce rates have fluctuated over the last forty years, falling in 2006 to 132,140, the lowest number of divorces since 1977. People who marry under the age of twenty-one are at most risk of divorce, as are those who remarry. The most common age for men and women to divorce is between twenty-five and twenty-nine, although there has been an increase in 'silver separation' – couples over the age of sixty getting divorced.

CALLING IT A DAY

According to UK divorce law:

You cannot get a divorce during the first year of marriage.

To apply for a divorce, either partner must prove in court that their marriage has 'irretrievably broken down' by proving one or more of the following: their partner has behaved unreasonably; they have lived apart for two years and both want to divorce; they have lived apart for five years and one of the partners wants a divorce; one of the partners has committed adultery; one of the partners has deserted the other two years prior to divorce application.

CHILDREN AND YOUNG FAMILIES

According to the 2011 census, there are just over 15 million children and young people aged nineteen and under living in the UK (just under one-quarter of the population). There are 3.5 million children under five in England and Wales, an increase of 406,000 since 2001, mainly due to higher fertility rates and a higher population of women of childbearing age as a result of migration.

Fewer parents are married and more children live with one parent. In 1996, 73 per cent of dependent children live with a married couple, compared to 62 per cent in 2012. Between 1996 and 2012, the number of dependent children living with opposite-sex non-married couples doubled from 0.9 million to 1.8 million. In 2012, 2 million single parents lived with dependent children, an increase of 0.4 million since 1996.

EDUCATION

Children between the ages of five and sixteen are required by law to receive full-time education, usually at school but they can be taught at home. From summer 2013, young people in England and Wales will be required to continue in school or training (such as an apprenticeship) until they turn seventeen, and from the summer of 2015 until they are eighteen. This is the first time the minimum age at which people can leave learning has been raised since 1972, when it was raised from fifteen to sixteen.

Schools in Britain are largely divided into state schools, funded by the taxpayer, and the independent sector, which is privately funded. The vast majority of children (94 per cent) go to state primary or secondary schools. Independent fee-paying schools cater for around 6.5 per cent of British children (7.2 per cent in England). The Education Act in 1944 reorganized schools in England and Wales (1947 in Scotland and Northern Ireland) after which most schools in England, Wales and Northern Ireland were divided into grammar schools, secondary modern schools and technical schools. Those who passed the eleven-plus examination went to grammar schools and those who failed went to the other schools. Labour governments from 1964 were increasingly committed to abolishing the selective school system, and introduced non-selective comprehensive schools. By 1975, the majority of local authorities in England and Wales had moved to the comprehensives systems and nearly all new schools were built as comprehensives. Currently around 90 per cent of pupils attend comprehensives, although 164 grammar schools remain in England and Wales. All state schools in Wales and Scotland are based on the comprehensive system, and Northern Ireland currently has a mixture of grammar schools and secondary schools, although the government has now abolished the eleven-plus transfer test.

In England and Scotland, pupils take the national Standard Attainment Test (Sats) at seven, eleven and fourteen years old (in Wales, national tests are taken at fourteen, with pupils facing teacher assessments at seven and eleven). At sixteen, most pupils in England, Wales and Northern Ireland take GCSEs (General Certificate of Secondary Education) and in Scotland NQs (National Qualifications). At seventeen and eighteen, many young people take AGCEs (Advanced General Certificates of Education, often referred to as A levels), AS level units, vocational qualifications or Higher/ Advanced Higher Grades in Scotland.

PRIVATE OR PUBLIC?

Some of the UK's most famous independent, fee-paying schools, such as Eton, Harrow and Winchester, are known, rather confusingly, as 'public schools'. The term dates back to the days when schools were controlled either by the Church or founded independently, the latter of which meant they lay outside of the control of ecclesiastical authority and were thus open to the paying public (the first of these schools was founded in around the late fourteenth and early fifteenth centuries).

From 1964 to 1997 every British prime minister, from Harold Wilson to John Major, was grammar-school educated. In 2011, half of the coalition cabinet and one-third of all MPs attended private school. A report by the Sutton Trust found that almost half of the new cabinet in 2015 had been privately educated (compared with 7 per cent of the general population), while there are 20 old Etonians now in the Commons, including Prime Minister David Cameron.

When Stephen Byers, former Labour Schools Minister, was interviewed on BBC Radio in 1998 about his plans to raise numeracy standards in schools, he was asked to multiply seven by eight. He answered fifty-four. Despite the blunder, a spokesman for the prime minister said he had full confidence in Mr Byers, stating, 'The prime minister and those responsible for government communications applaud anything which gets up in lights the issues we are seeking to promote.'

After school, one in three young people go on to further education at college or university. People may choose to go on to university, a college of further education or an adult education centre, which offer both academic and vocational courses.

In 1960, there were twenty-two British universities. There are now 116 universities, following expansion in the 1960s and reforms in 1992 that granted university status to polytechnics.

Competition to enter university is very strong. An average of 17 per cent of students drop out of further education because of financial or other problems.

Prior to 1998, anyone who gained a place at an institution of higher education was awarded a grant from local education authorities. The grant covered tuition fees and, subject to parental income, living costs (rent, books etc.). In 1998, this was abolished and students, other than in Scotland, now have to pay tuition fees, although students from less affluent backgrounds don't have to pay the full amount. Students must pay for their own living costs, usually through loans provided by a student loan company. Most students will finish their studies with an average debt of £44,000.

> 'The Minister for School Standards and myself [sic] meet regularly with those parent's [sic], teacher's [sic] and head's [sic] who have a commitment to raising standards.'
>
> A DEPARTMENT FOR EDUCATION PARLIAMENTARY PAPER DRAFTED BY OFFICIALS IN FEBRUARY 2001 UNDER THE NAME OF DAVID BLUNKETT, FORMER SECRETARY OF STATE FOR EDUCATION.

THE EMPLOYMENT OF CHILDREN

The main law concerning the employment of children under sixteen is the Children and Young Persons Act 1933, which sets fourteen as the minimum age at which children can be employed. There are also countless other relevant pieces of legislation and local authorities vary on the types and duration of work children can undertake. The 1933 Act stipulates that a fourteen-year-old should not work during school hours, or for more than five hours on a Saturday or any other day in the school holidays, and for only two hours on a Sunday. The national minimum wage does not apply to workers under the age of sixteen.

'It has been said that children should be kept at school until fourteen years of age; but the amount and importance of the labour which lads between ten and fourteen can perform should not be ignored. Since the present educational system has come into operation, the weeds have very much multiplied in Norfolk, which was once regarded as quite the garden of England, weeding being particularly the work of children whose labour is cheap, whose sight is keen, bodies flexible and fingers nimble.'

LIBERAL POLITICIAN EARL FORTESCUE (1854–1932), 1880.

WOMEN AT WORK AND MOTHERHOOD

'She wasn't an ardent feminist. She was very beautiful.'

LABOUR MP NORMAN BUCHAN IN 1988, ON
THE DEATH OF LABOUR MP JENNIE LEE.

Opportunities for women at work have improved although many would argue that inequalities are still in force. On average, girls leave school with better qualifications than boys and women now outnumber men at university. However, after leaving university, most women earn less than men and the average hourly rate paid to women is 20 per cent less.

Britain has an increasing percentage of working mothers and wives – women are returning more quickly to work after the birth of a child and, as a whole, make up 45 per cent of the workforce.

Women are also delaying having children. In 2011, the average age of a woman at the birth of her first child was twenty-eight, and nearly half of all babies are born to women aged thirty or older. More women are also having babies in their forties. In 2011, 30,000 women over forty had babies, which is three times the amount twenty years ago.

The number of young mothers under the age of twenty fell by 29 per cent between 2001 and 2011. In 2009, the rate of teenage pregnancy was the lowest it had been since 1999, although figures in 2010 showed that Britain still has the highest unmarried teenage pregnancy rate in Western Europe.

The law in the UK states that men and women who do the same job should receive equal pay. It is also unlawful for a person to be refused work, training or promotion because of their sex, nationality or ethnicity, religion, disability, sexual orientation or age (or, in Northern Ireland, political opinion).

WOMEN ON TOP

No woman in my time will be Prime Minister or Chancellor or Foreign Secretary – not the top jobs. Anyway, I wouldn't want to be Prime Minister. You have to give yourself 100 per cent.'

MARGARET THATCHER IN *THE SUNDAY TELEGRAPH* ON 26 OCTOBER 1969, ON APPOINTMENT AS SHADOW EDUCATION SPOKESMAN.

Just a few months later, Thatcher was appointed Secretary for Education and Science in Edward Heath's government. She became Leader of the Opposition in 1975 and prime minister in 1979.

In 2006, Margaret Beckett was appointed Foreign Secretary by Tony Blair, becoming the first woman to hold the post. There haven't, as yet, been any female Chancellors and the UK still lags behind many Western democracies in terms of the number of women in its cabinet. There are currently seven women in the twenty-two-strong cabinet, just 31 per cent.

RELIGION

'I'm sorry. We don't do God.'

FORMER PRESS SECRETARY ALASTAIR CAMPBELL IN 2003, AFTER PM TONY BLAIR WAS ASKED ABOUT HIS CHRISTIAN FAITH BY *VANITY FAIR*.

The UK is historically a Christian country although anyone living in the country is free to practise any religion (or none at all) and religious discrimination is unlawful. In the UK-wide 2001 census, around 72 per cent of the population (37.3 million) said they were Christian. In the 2011 census for England and Wales, 59 per cent of the population (33.2 million) stated they were Christian; one-quarter of the population said they had no religion at all (rising from 15 per cent in 2001); Muslims represented the next largest percentage of the population at 2.7 million.

NSO England and Wales 2011 census showing religious diversity:

Muslims .... 2.7 million
Hindu 817,000
Sikh 423,000
Jewish 263,000
Buddhist 248,000

Other religions, including pagan and spiritualist: 240,000

According to the 2011 census for England and Wales, Wales has the highest proportion of people who claim not to be religious (one-third of the population), and Norwich is the local authority with the highest proportion of people with no religion (42.5 per cent). London is the most diverse region in terms of religious affiliation, with the highest proportion of Muslims (12 per cent of London's total population).

IRREGULAR

In 2007, of the people who said they were Christian only around 10 per cent attended church weekly and two-thirds had not gone to church in the past week. Today, retired people make up an estimated 42 per cent of Christian congregations (with people under fifty-five opting for more evangelical religions).

In the UK, Christianity is a composite of the Church of England (the Anglican Church), the Roman Catholic Church, the Church of Scotland and the Free Churches (which include Nonconformist Protestant denominations like the Methodist Church and the Salvation Army).

THE CHURCH OF ENGLAND

The official Church in England is the Church of England (as established in the 1530s, see page 46). The monarch is the head of the Church; its archbishops, bishops and deans are appointed by the monarch on the advice of the prime minister. The most senior bishop of the Church of England and professional head of the Church is the Archbishop of Canterbury (called the Primate of All England); he is the metropolitan of the southern province of England (the province of Canterbury). The second most senior bishop is the Archbishop of York, the metropolitan of the northern province of England (the province of York). The two archbishops, along with twenty-four senior bishops, sit in the House of Lords and are the Church's link with Parliament.

Rowan Williams was Archbishop of Canterbury from 2002 until 31 December 2012. Justin Welby succeeded him in early 2013 and Ugandan John Sentamu has been the Archbishop of York since 2005.

In October 2007, Sentamu was awarded the Yorkshireman of the Year title. During his speech he joked about the African-Yorkshire DNA connection, particularly as his middle name 'Mugabi' spelled backwards is 'ibagum' (a well-known expression of shock in northern England).

The provinces of York and Canterbury are divided into forty-four dioceses, each of which is under the control of a bishop. These dioceses are then divided into 13,000 parishes, most of which have a priest (also called a vicar or a rector) in charge.

The Church does not receive any direct government support – most of its resources come from substantial property and investments. It is the third largest landowner in Britain after the Crown and the Forestry Commission.

In 1994, the General Synod (the legislative body of the Church that can create two types of legislation: measures that have to be approved but cannot be amended by Parliament before receiving the Royal Assent, and canon laws that are the law of the Church requiring only Royal Licence) approved the ordination of women as priests. In 2014, the General Synod voted to allow women to become bishops, for the first time in its history, with its first female bishop, the Right Reverend Libby Lane, ordained in 2015.

NUMBERLAND

In 2010, there were 8,087 ordained men compared to 3,535 women. However, during that year, and for the first time, the number of women joining the Church as priests outnumbered men, with 290 women ordained in comparison to 273 men.

'When I'm sitting on the woolsack in the House of Lords, I amuse myself by saying "bollocks" sotto voce to the bishops.'

LORD HAILSHAM (1907–2001), LORD CHANCELLOR, 1985.

Another area of controversy is the issue over whether priests can be openly gay or in practising homosexual relationships. In January 2013, the Church of England dropped its ban on allowing openly gay clergy to become bishops, so long as they promised to remain celibate. The new ruling reopened the bitter debate between the conservative and liberal wings of the Church with conservative Anglicans arguing that the ruling will cause significant rifts.

THE CHURCH OF SCOTLAND

Commonly known as the Kirk, the Church of Scotland is Presbyterian Protestant and free from state control. It was created in 1560 by John Knox, who followed the teachings of John Calvin, the leading exponent of the European Reformation. It has no bishops and individual churches are governed by a minster (which includes women) and elders at a Kirk Session. The supreme organizational body of the Church is the General Assembly, which is chaired by the Church's most senior representative, the Moderator. Wales and Northern Ireland do not have established churches.

OTHER DENOMINATIONS

Catholicism is widely practised throughout Britain (in 2009, there were 5 million nominal members of the Roman Catholic faith in England and Wales) with regular weekly observance of just over 1 million. The head of the Catholic Church in England is the Cardinal Archbishop in Westminster and the senior lay Catholic is the Duke of Norfolk. There are seven Roman Catholic provinces in the UK (four in England, two in Scotland and one in Wales) each under the jurisdiction of an archbishop; bishops oversee each of the thirty dioceses and there are 3,000 parishes.

The Free Churches are Nonconformist Protestant denominations. The Methodist Church is the largest Free Church (and the UK's fourth largest Church), with (in

2007) a community of around 800,000 who have an active involvement in the Church. Other Free Churches include the Baptist Union, the United Reformed Church, and the Salvation Army.

The Jewish community is divided into the Orthodox faith (the majority faith in the UK) led by the Chief Rabbi, alongside Reform and Liberal groups. Around two-thirds of Jews in the United Kingdom live in Greater London. There are 300 local synagogues in the UK and one in three Jewish children attend Jewish schools. The representative body for all Jews in the UK is the Board of Deputies of British Jews.

There are increasing numbers of Muslims in the UK and religious observance is higher than in other groups. The Muslim Council of Britain was formed in 1997 and represents all British Muslims. The vast majority of British Muslims live in England and Wales and there are more than 1,500 mosques in the UK.

There are around 200 Sikh temples in the UK and 143 Hindu temples.

In England and Wales, non-denominational Christian worship is compulsory in state primary and secondary schools. Schools are required to hold daily religious assemblies although in practice few do. In addition, all schools must provide RE (religious education) to its pupils, which must have a Christian basis but also cover other major religions. Parents are allowed to take their children out of these lessons.

HEALTH

'That's enough health, I need a fag.'

CHARLES KENNEDY (1959–2015), FORMER LEADER OF THE
LIBERAL DEMOCRATS (AUGUST 1999 TO JANUARY 2006) AND
THEN LIBERAL DEMOCRAT SPOKESMAN, OVERHEARD AFTER
POSING FOR PHOTOGRAPHERS WHILE PROMOTING HEALTHY
FOOD AT A GLASGOW SUPERMARKET, JUNE 1999.

THE NATIONAL HEALTH SERVICE

The National Health Service (NHS) in Britain is now one of the largest organizations in Europe and is the biggest single employer of people in Western Europe. Launched in the UK in 1948, it established a system of free healthcare and treatment for all UK residents. Prior to 1948, patients were generally required to pay for their medical care.

The NHS was originally intended to be completely free for all, although patients now pay for prescriptions, dental work and eye tests. However, GP (General Practitioner) services are free, as are hospital and most medical treatments for British and EU citizens. There are around 35,000 GPs in the UK, who have an average of 2,000 registered patients.

The UK government funds the NHS through taxes and National Insurance systems, and is responsible for the NHS in England through the Department of Health. Scotland, Wales and Northern Ireland handle their own health matters through their devolved authorities.

The NHS also shares some facilities and healthcare

treatment with institutions owned and financed by the private sector. A quarter of all operations and healthcare in the UK are paid for by patients or financed through private healthcare insurance policies. However, most expensive, long-term care is conducted by the NHS.

ILLNESS AND DEATH

'People in the north die of ignorance and crisps.'

FORMER CONSERVATIVE MP EDWINA CURRIE, TWO WEEKS AFTER
BECOMING JUNIOR HEATH MINISTER, SEPTEMBER 1986.

While life expectancy in the UK has continued to rise – in 2010, the average life expectancy for men was 78.2 years and for women 82.3 years – there is a widening gap between areas with the lowest and highest life expectancies, attributed to differences in social class, income, economic deprivation and health. Life expectancy is highest in England, particularly in southern England, and lowest in Scotland. The London borough of Kensington and Chelsea has the highest life-expectancy rates, with men living to 85.1 years and women to 87.8 years. Glasgow was identified as having the lowest life expectancy, with men living to 71.6 years and women 78 years.

AIDS

'There will be one million AIDS cases in Britain by the end of 1991.'

WORLD HEALTH ORGANIZATION REPORT, JULY 1989.

AIDS (acquired immunodeficiency syndrome) was first recognized in the UK as a notifiable disease in 1984. By June 1993 there were 7,699 reported AIDS cases in the UK. At the end of 2011 there were around 96,000 people living with HIV, of whom one-quarter were unaware of the infection.

'Suicide is a real threat to health in a modern society.'

FORMER CONSERVATIVE HEALTH SECRETARY
VIRGINIA BOTTOMLEY, C. 1993.

Men are more likely to commit suicide than women. In 2011, 4,552 men committed suicide compared to 1,493 women, with the highest suicide rate among males aged thirty to forty-four (23.5 deaths out of a population of 100,000). Between 2007 and 2011, the suicide rate in males aged forty-five to fifty-nine also increased significantly (22.2 deaths per 100,000 population) and the Department of Health identified middle-aged men – particularly those from poorer socio-economic backgrounds who live on their own – as one of the high-risk groups for suicide prevention. London still has the lowest male suicide rate, the north-east the highest.

TRANSPORT

For a relatively small island, Britain's transport network is considerable.

THE ROADS

The road is the most popular method of transport in the UK, with car travel accounting for 80 per cent of passenger journeys. At the end of 2011, there were 34.2 million licensed vehicles in the UK. Since 1937, roads have been funded by general taxation, although there are some tolls for major bridges and tunnels and the UK's first toll motorway, the M6 Toll around Birmingham, opened in 2003. Congestion charging also operates in London and Durham. Britain has a very high road density, with an 80 per cent increase in traffic since 1980.

THE RULES OF THE ROAD

You need to own a UK or EU driving licence to drive on public roads in the UK. If you have a licence from outside the EU, you can drive in the UK for up to twelve months, but thereon you need to secure a UK driving licence. To drive a car or a motorcycle, you should be aged seventeen or over; to drive a medium-sized lorry, eighteen, and to drive a large bus or lorry, twenty-one.

Speed limits for cars and motorcycles:

- 30 mph in built-up areas (unless a sign says differently)
- 60 mph on single carriageways
- 70 mph on motorways and dual carriageways

UK law requires you to:

- Wear a seat belt in the car (children under twelve may require a booster seat)
- Wear a crash helmet on a motorcycle (although this doesn't apply to Sikh men wearing a turban)
- Not to hold a mobile phone while driving
- Not to drive away without stopping if you are involved in a road accident

THE RAIL SYSTEM

The UK's rail system is the oldest in the world, home to the first ever public railway, which opened in 1825 between Stockton and Darlington (see page 56). In 1948, the rail network was nationalized to form British Railways, latterly British Rail. In the 1960s, due to declining profits, the government gave Dr Richard Beeching the task of reorganizing the railway. The Beeching Report, popularly known as the Beeching Axe, led to the closure of 4,000 miles of route lines. In 1997, the rail network was privatized, with Railtrack (later Network Rail) in ownership of the lines and infrastructure, and private companies in ownership of the trains and stations.

Since 1995, passenger numbers have been increasing, from approximately 975.5 million rail journeys in 2002–3, to more than 1.5 billion journeys in 2012–13. Ticket prices, however, are some of the highest in the world.

The Northern Ireland rail network is publicly owned by Northern Ireland Railways (NIR). It is connected to the Republic of Ireland, and is one of the few networks in Europe to carry no freight.

The London Underground

'You have your own company, your own temperature control, your own music, and you don't have to put up with dreadful human beings sitting alongside you.'

STEVEN NORRIS, FORMER CONSERVATIVE MINISTER OF TRANSPORT, COMPARING CARS TO PUBLIC TRANSPORT IN A COMMENT TO THE COMMONS ENVIRONMENT SELECT COMMITTEE, FEBRUARY 1995.

The London Underground system (commonly referred to by Londoners as the Tube) comprises 249 miles of track and 270 stations, and is the fourth largest metro system in the world after Seoul Metropolitan Subway, the Shanghai Metro and the Beijing Subway. In 2011 and 2012, passenger journeys numbered 1.2 billion. The system comprises eleven lines: Bakerloo, Central, Circle, District, Hammersmith & City, Jubilee, Metropolitan, Northern, Piccadilly, Victoria and Waterloo & City.

The Tube began service on 10 January 1863, covering a three-and-a-half mile journey between Paddington and Farringdon on the Metropolitan line.

The top five busiest stations on the London Underground network are: Waterloo (84.12 million users in 2011), Victoria (82.25 million users), King's Cross St Pancras (77.11 million), Oxford Circus (77.09 million) and Liverpool Street (63.65 million).

The London Underground map evolved from a design by electrical engineer Harry Beck in 1933. Its colour-coded, schematic layout, with the location of stations mapped in relation to each other, rather than geographically, has evolved into a design classic and has been adopted by map designers across the world.

Other metropolitan underground and rail systems in the UK are the Glasgow Subway and the Tyne and Wear Metro.

'A very friendly boom, like a pair of gleeful handclaps.'

IN 1971, THEN UK GOVERNMENT SCIENTIFIC ADVISER SIR JAMES
LIGHTHILL DISMISSES THE IDEA THAT THE NEW PASSENGER AIRLINE
CONCORDE MIGHT BE NOISY. THE PROTOTYPE'S BREAKING OF THE
SOUND BARRIER IS DESCRIBED BY WITNESSES AS LIKE 'FLYING BOMBS
LANDING HALF A MILE AWAY'.

GATWICK

There are 471 airports and airfields in the UK. London's
Heathrow Airport is the biggest airport in the UK and one
of the busiest, in terms of traffic volume, in the world. It is
owned by BAA, the UK's largest airport operator, which
in 2009 was ordered by the Competition Commission
to sell three airports to promote competition. The UK's
second largest airport is Gatwick, now owned by Global
Infrastructure Partners, followed by Manchester Airport,
which is run by the Manchester Airport Group.

PORTS

Most freight (95 per cent) enters Britain by sea, with the
majority of traffic journeying through Felixstowe in Suffolk
(which deals with around 40 per cent of UK freight trade),
Tilbury on the River Thames, and Southampton on the
south coast. Dover is the busiest ferry port in the UK and
Europe.

ENERGY SUPPLIES

The main energy sources in the UK are oil, gas, nuclear power, hydroelectric power and coal. Until around 2005, the UK was almost self-sufficient in energy supplies due to the extraction of offshore gas and oil supplies from the North Sea and the Atlantic. However, the country now has a heavier dependence on imported foreign gas and oil – in the winter of 2009–10, it relied on imports for half its gas supplies – and the search for alternative forms of energy is now a crucial issue.

There are currently nine nuclear plants in the UK generating around one-sixth of the country's electricity. Calder Hall in Cumbria was the first nuclear power station, which began operation in 1956. The most recently constructed nuclear plant is the Sizewell B plant in Suffolk, which began producing power in 1995. In 2010, the coalition government gave the go-ahead for eight new nuclear power stations as part of a wide-ranging plan to keep up with the UK's energy needs, while reducing carbon emissions by 80 per cent by 2050. Scotland, however, has since announced it will block any building of nuclear plants north of the border and in 2012 two of the big six power companies in the UK confirmed they would be pulling out of developing nuclear plants.

The burning of coal in the 1940s provided 90 per cent of the UK's energy. During the 1980s and 1990s, the industry was scaled back considerably by the Thatcher government with the closure of many of the uneconomic pits and the privatization of the industry. Currently 30 per cent of the UK's electricity is generated from coal-fired power stations (and 70 per cent of the coal used to generate the nation's energy is imported from places like Russia and South Africa).

Electricity generation by wind power is now in use in the UK, with 362 wind farms and 4,896 wind turbines currently operating. The UK has the largest offshore wind farm in the world – the Thanet wind farm off the Kent coast. Wind power is expected to continue growing in the UK over the foreseeable future and in 2010 the coalition government announced plans to build 44,000 wind turbines around the coast and to encourage households to put up solar panels in a commitment to renewable energy.

'But will they ever produce enough electricity to make the turbines go round?'

PRINCE PHILIP, DISCUSSING WIND POWER DURING
A VISIT TO THE ROYAL SOCIETY IN MAY 2001.

CRIME

A subject of much debate, crime in the UK is always big news.

THE POLICE

The police force's role is to maintain law and order in the UK. According to *The Guardian*, in September 2012 there were 132,235 policemen and women operating in the UK. The force is made up of fifty-two regional forces, each headed by a chief constable. The Metropolitan Police is the largest force (employing, in 2011, 31,478 officers) and is responsible for law enforcement in Greater London from its headquarters in Scotland Yard.

BOBBY ON THE BEAT

Sir Robert Peel created the first police force, known as the 'bobbies' or the 'peelers', in 1829 in Ireland while serving as Home Secretary. The tall dome-shaped helmet, which was adopted by the Met Police in 1863 to replace the stovepipe top hat, is still worn by many police officers in England and Wales when on foot patrol. The uniform of the Police Service of Northern Ireland (PSNI) is very different to the British uniform, its main colour being dark and light green.

'There are more crimes in Britain now, due to the huge
rise in the crime rate.'

NEIL KINNOCK, FORMER LEADER OF THE LABOUR PARTY,
ON BBC RADIO IN 1985.

The police have to obey a set of rules when arresting someone. They must identify themselves as the police and explain why they are arresting someone (providing an interpreter if that person doesn't speak English). The police can use 'reasonable force' (such as handcuffs) if a person resists arrest, and they also have powers to search the arrestee. They normally can't interview a person under the age of seventeen without the presence of a parent or appropriate adult.

Those arrested or detained at a police station have important legal rights, including: access to free legal advice; the right to send a message to someone telling them where they are; the right to medical help, if necessary; the right to see the Codes of Practice, the rules the police must follow.

The following official police caution is also given to all suspects:

'You do not have to say anything. But it may harm your defence if you do not mention, when questioned, something which you later rely on in court. Anything you do say may be given in evidence.'

HER MAJESTY'S PRISONS

In England and Wales, the prison population has risen steadily since 1945, surpassing 80,000 for the first time in 2006 and exceeding the operational capacity of the prison system. By July 2012, seventy-seven prisons in England and Wales (59 per cent) were overcrowded and at the end of 2011 the prison population in England and Wales was at a record high with a total of 88,179 prisoners (4,200 of whom were female). At the end of March 2013, the prison population had declined to 83,769. In Scotland, the prison population reached its highest level ever recorded at 8,178 in March 2012.

In 2009, the UK had 151 prisoners per 100,000 of the population, the second highest rate in Western Europe, below Spain. The US has the highest rate in the developed world (748) while Iceland has the lowest (55).

According to the 2012 House of Commons prison population figures (for England and Wales and a limited analysis of Scottish prisons), over 25 per cent of prisoners were taken into care as a child, compared to 2 per cent of the population as a whole; 43 per cent of prisoners had a family member convicted of a criminal offence; two-thirds of prisoners had numeracy skills at or below the level expected of an eleven-year-old. One half of male prisoners and seven out of ten female prisoners have no school qualifications.

THE ECONOMY

'It needs to be said that the poor are poor because they don't have enough money.'

KEITH JOSEPH (1918–94), THEN CONSERVATIVE SECRETARY OF STATE FOR SOCIAL SERVICES, 1970.

The UK has a mixed economy, with over two-thirds of companies in the private sector and one-third in the state sector (most state-run companies were privatized after 1979). The Bank of England is the UK's central bank, and is responsible for setting interest rates. The government department known as the Treasury exercises control over the British economy and is headed by the Chancellor of the Exchequer. The Bank of England works to inflation targets set by the government, and if the governor of the Bank fails to deliver he sends a letter to the Chancellor explaining why.

CHEQUERED

The government department responsible for collecting tax and revenue is known as the Exchequer. The word 'exchequer' refers to an early medieval cloth used to perform calculations for taxes and the king's revenue. Draped over a table, its chequered pattern resembled a chessboard (*echiquier* in French).

Britain is currently the world's sixth largest economy. In 2009, 75 per cent of its GDP (gross domestic product) was derived from services and 23.8 per cent from manufacturing and industry, highlighting the importance of the service sector (retail, tourism etc.) in the UK's economy and the decline of traditional sources of wealth in manufacturing and industry. The UK also has a significant globalized economy: London, alongside New York, is the world's largest financial centre.

ILL-MATCHED

'There are two problems in my life. The political ones are insoluble and the economic ones are incomprehensible.'

ALEC DOUGLAS-HOME (1903–95),
CONSERVATIVE POLITICIAN AND FORMER PRIME MINISTER IN 1964.

Despite having held a series of senior posts in government, including Leader of the House of Lords, Foreign Secretary and prime minister (but, thankfully, not Chancellor), Alec Douglas-Home was no economist. In an interview in 1962, he admitted he had to do his sums with the aid of matchsticks.

'Dear Chief Secretary, I'm afraid to tell you there's no money left.'

LIAM BYRNE, LABOUR POLITICIAN AND FORMER CHIEF SECRETARY
TO THE TREASURY, IN A LETTER TO HIS SUCCESSOR, DAVID LAWS, AS
QUOTED BY LAWS, 17 MAY 2010.

Between 2007 and 2010, as part of the worst global recession since the Great Depression of 1929 (see page 63), Britain's economy weakened. As economic structures around the world faced collapse, the UK government was forced to hand out bailouts to banks such as Northern Rock and the Royal Bank of Scotland (which remain partly state-owned). This led to a major budget deficit of £163 billion, which the government is currently trying to reduce with major cuts to public spending.

'Inflation ... is currently running at 8.4 per cent.'

DENIS HEALEY, RETIRED LABOUR MP AND THEN CHANCELLOR
OF THE EXCHEQUER, IN A PRESS CONFERENCE IN SEPTEMBER 1974.
THE FIGURE WAS, IN FACT, WIDELY OFF THE MARK –
THE ACTUAL RATE WAS 15.6 PER CENT.

THE BUDGET BOX

Every year on budget day – the day upon which the government presents its budget to a legislature – the Chancellor of the Exchequer appears on the steps of 11 Downing Street and displays for photographers the 'Budget box', which contains his budget statement.

The famous red leather briefcase was first made for William Gladstone in around 1860 and used until Gordon Brown ordered a new one in 1997. (Alistair Darling, Brown's successor, reverted to using the Gladstone bag, but current Chancellor George Osborne has plumped for the new one.) In March 2013, Osborne tweeted a picture of his cat 'Freya' sitting inside the briefcase, and, unlike his handling of the economy, the post was met with general delight and described by journalist Iain Martin as 'innovative'.

'I never could make out what those damned dots meant.'

LORD RANDOLPH CHURCHILL (1911–68), FORMER CHANCELLOR OF THE EXCHEQUER AND FATHER OF WINSTON CHURCHILL, ON DECIMAL POINTS, 1906.

TAX

Funds for central government are raised from taxes, in the form of income tax, National Insurance contributions, VAT (value added tax), corporation tax and fuel duty. Income tax is payable on paid employment, pensions, property, savings and dividends, and is the single largest source of revenue for the government, financing things such as roads, education, the armed forces and the police. The second largest source of revenue for the government are National Insurance contributions, which covers state benefits and services such as the NHS and the State Pension, and towards which almost everyone who works contributes. Tax rates set by Parliament apply throughout the UK, but the Scottish Parliament has the power to alter income tax rates in Scotland by up to 3p in the pound.

'CORRUPTION WINS NOT MORE THAN HONESTY': GOVERNMENT

'There's a lot of bleeding idiots in t'country, and they deserve some representation.'

BILL STONES (1904–69), LABOUR MP FOR DURHAM.

HOW IT ALL WORKS

The United Kingdom is a constitutional monarchy and a parliamentary democracy with the Queen reigning as Head of State under constitutional limitations.

THE CONSTITUTION

A constitution, in which the powers, principles and institutions of the state are defined and laid out, is in many countries written into a single document. The UK has an 'unwritten' constitution because its practice of government, laws and institutions have evolved over several centuries, and are not written down in one document (although much of it is written down in laws passed in Parliament). Countries like the US and France have single, written constitutions largely because revolutions led to entirely new systems of government.

PARLIAMENTARY SOVEREIGNTY

Parliamentary sovereignty is a key principle of the UK constitution. Parliament, which consists of the House of Commons, the House of Lords and, formally, the monarch, has supreme legal authority in the UK, creating or ending any law. Generally, the courts cannot overrule its legislation.

THE GOVERNMENT

The UK is currently divided into 650 parliamentary constituencies, each of which is represented by one MP (Member of Parliament) in the House of Commons. MPs help to create new laws, debate important national issues and represent the concerns of their constituency. The average number of voters in each constituency is 66,250, although this varies widely across the country.

General elections are held at least every five years and the party with the largest number of MPs in the House of Commons (i.e. secures more than half the seats in the Commons – 326) forms the government. The party that wins the second largest number of seats becomes the main opposition party. If no party wins an overall majority, this is known as a hung parliament.

INDECISIVE

'England does not love coalitions.'

BENJAMIN DISRAELI (1804–81), CONSERVATIVE
POLITICIAN AND PRIME MINISTER, IN 1852.

In the 2010 General Election, no single party won an overall majority (the first time in the UK since February 1974). The Conservatives won the most seats, at 306, Labour won 258 seats, and the Liberal Democrats won 57 seats. On 11 May 2010, the Conservatives and the Liberal Democrats agreed to form a coalition government. After five years of compromises with the Conservatives, the Liberal Democrats suffered a humiliating defeat in the 2015 general election and were shown the door as the Conservatives formed their majority government.

IT'S A DATE

The Fixed-Term Parliaments Act of 2011 stipulated that general elections would be held on the first Thursday in May every five years, which meant the prime minister could no longer choose the date of a general election. However, an election can be triggered if a motion of no confidence in the government is passed by a simple majority of MPs (50 per cent plus 1) or a motion for a general election is agreed by two-thirds of the total number of seats in the Commons.

THE MONARCHY

'It is obvious I shall have to abandon my hopes of getting the Queen's head off the stamps.'

TONY BENN (1925–2014), FORMER LABOUR POLITICIAN AND MP, 1965.

The monarch is the head of state for the UK, head of the Executive, Judiciary and Legislature, Supreme Governor of the Church of England and commander-in-chief of the armed forces. The Queen is also the Head of the Commonwealth and head of state in fifteen of the fifty-three Commonwealth member countries. The Queen appoints the government, and Acts of Parliament and the business of state are carried out in her name, although her role is largely ceremonial and actual political power is exercised by others. The monarch is only sovereign by the will of Parliament and the acceptance of the people.

The monarchy is expected to be politically neutral and is not allowed to make laws or impose taxes and acts only on the advice of government ministers.

The Queen performs important ceremonial duties such as the opening of the new parliamentary session each year, during which she reads the 'Queen's Speech', in which she states the government agenda for the forthcoming year. She also officially appoints the prime minister after a general election and gives letters of appointment to other officials within the government, armed forces and the Church of England (always on the advice of the prime minister). She has weekly meetings with the prime minister during which time she can privately discuss matters of government.

Succession rules decree that elder children inherit the crown before younger siblings, and only Protestants can become king or queen. In 2012, new legislation was agreed allowing anyone in the line of succession to marry a Roman Catholic (which had been formerly banned) and also ending male-preference primogeniture, under which sons had taken precedence over daughters in the line of succession.

CROWNING GLORY

The current monarch is Queen Elizabeth II. She was born on 21 April 1926, the first child of the Duke and Duchess of York (later King George VI and queen consort) and was named Elizabeth Alexandra Mary (close family calling her 'Lillibet'). Following her father's death, Elizabeth was proclaimed queen on 6 February 1952, with her coronation taking place on 2 June 1953. She is married to Prince Philip, Duke of Edinburgh, and has four children: Charles, Anne, Andrew and Edward. She celebrated her Diamond Jubilee in 2012. The Queen's eldest son, Prince Charles, is heir to the throne.

The Queen has given regular audiences to twelve prime ministers, which began with Winston Churchill. There have been seven Archbishops of Canterbury during the Queen's reign (Geoffrey Fisher, Michael Ramsey, Donald Coggan, Robert Runcie, George Carey, Rowan Williams and Justin Welby).

GB FACT

New citizens affirm or swear loyalty to the Queen as part of the citizenship ceremony.

As well as her actual birthday on 21 April, the Queen has an official birthday, which is celebrated in the UK on a Saturday in June. The day is marked by the Trooping the Colour ceremony, which is held on Horse Guards Parade in Whitehall, London, by the Household Division (Foot Guards and Household Cavalry), along with the announcement of birthday honours.

WITH GREAT HONOUR

The honours system rewards exceptional achievement in public life and service to the UK. Candidates can be nominated by the public or government departments, and are selected by an independent committee, then submitted to the prime minister for approval, before being sent to the sovereign for final authorization. The Queen or her royal representatives present the awards at a ceremony, most often at Buckingham Palace.

The role of the monarchy is frequently criticized, many seeing it as an out-of-date, undemocratic and expensive institution, although it remains relatively popular among the British people. In 2013, a MORI poll found that 77 per cent of respondents wanted to retain the monarchy, while 17 per cent would prefer an elected head of state.

WILLIAM AND CATHERINE

The Queen's grandson Prince William is second in line to the British throne (after his father, Charles, Prince of Wales) and is one of the most popular figures in the royal family. The first son of Diana, Princess of Wales, he was born on 21 June 1982 and named William Arthur Philip Louis Windsor. His brother, Harry, was born two years later in 1984. By 1992 his parents' marriage had irretrievably broken down, leading to divorce in 1996. A year later, on 31 August, Diana died in a car crash in Paris (also killing her companion, Dodi Fayed, and her driver). In 2005, Charles married former girlfriend Camilla Parker Bowles. After schooling at Eton and a year spent travelling, William attended the University of St Andrews in Scotland where he studied History of Art and, later, geography, graduating in 2005. There, he met Catherine 'Kate' Middleton. He entered the Royal Military Academy in Sandhurst in 2006 and is currently a member of the Royal Air Force working as a search-and-rescue helicopter pilot. On 29 April 2011, he married Kate Middleton at Westminister Abbey, becoming Duke of Cambridge, Earl of Strathearn and Baron Carrickfergus.

Catherine Elizabeth Middleton was born on 9 January 1982, the eldest of three children. Her parents Michael and Carole run a successful children's party supplies company, and sent Kate to Marlborough boarding college where she excelled in sports and academia. In 2001, Kate went to the University of St Andrews to study History of Art during which time she began dating Prince William. Years of media scrutiny (the papers dubbing her 'Waity Katy') finally led to an engagement to William in 2010 and marriage the following year, whereupon she took the title Duchess of Cambridge. On 22 July 2013, Kate gave birth to the couple's first child, and the third in line to the throne, George Alexander Louis, and their daughter, Charlotte Elizabeth Diana, was born on 2 May 2015.

GB FACT

When meeting the Queen, the correct form of address is 'Your Majesty' and subsequently 'Ma'am' (as in 'jam'). For male members of the royal family, the title first used is 'Your Royal Highness' and subsequently 'Sir'. There is no obligation to bow or curtsy but traditional etiquette is for women to make a small curtsy and men a head bow.

THE GOVERNMENT

THE PRIME MINISTER

The prime minister is the head of the UK government and, as such, is responsible for all governmental policy and decisions and the appointment of members of the government. The prime minister is based at 10 Downing Street in Whitehall, London, and has a considerable staff of civil servants (see page 163) and personal advisers. He or she also has a country residence known as Chequers in Buckinghamshire.

A prime minister can lose his or her premiership if MPs in the governing party vote or pass a motion of no confidence, or if they choose to resign.

NOT IN MY NAME

The title 'Prime Minister' exists only by convention and is not actually established by any constitution or law. (The incumbent, therefore, should be referred to as 'the prime minister', not 'Prime Minister', as it is a position, not a title.) Although it has existed *de facto* for centuries, its first mention in official state documents didn't occur until the beginning of the twentieth century. The prime minister's legal authority is derived primarily from the fact that he or she is also the First Lord of the Treasury.

THE CABINET

The Cabinet is an executive committee composed of the prime minister and approximately twenty senior politicians, all of whom meet weekly to decide on the general policies of government. Cabinet ministers are heads of government departments, and include the Home Secretary, Foreign Secretary, Chancellor of the Exchequer and other ministers responsible for areas such as defence, education and health. The word 'cabinet' derives from the small room used to give counsel to the monarch, and in constitutional terms the Cabinet is a committee of Her Majesty's Most Honourable Privy Council and its ministers are entitled to use the prefix 'The Right Honourable'.

THE HOUSE OF COMMONS

'Anyone who enjoys being in the House of Commons probably needs psychiatric help.'

LABOUR POLITICIAN AND FORMER
MAYOR OF LONDON, KEN LIVINGSTONE.

The House of Commons is the centre of political debate and power in the UK, sharing the palace of Westminster with the House of Lords. Within the Commons, the prime minister and elected MPs consider and propose new laws and scrutinize government policy, and, since the Parliament Act of 1911, is the more dominant branch of Parliament (with the House of Lords permitted only to delay most legislation for a maximum of three parliamentary sessions or two calendar years). The House of Commons is sometimes referred to as the Lower House and the House of Lords as the Upper House (which in medieval times was the more powerful of the two).

In the House of Commons rival parties sit on opposite benches and in the past were deliberately positioned two sword lengths apart as a precaution against things getting out of hand. Debate in the House of Commons can often become heated, with either side jeering, taunting and cheering, stamping their feet and fluttering order papers.

MPs, however, are obliged to abide by a set of ancient rules enforced by the speaker of the House of Commons. These are:

- MPs do not refer to their colleagues by name but must refer to each other as 'honourable members'

- To speak in the House of Commons, MPs must 'catch the speaker's eye' by rising or half-rising from their seat in order to get the speaker's attention

- When a new speaker is elected to the House of Commons, he or she is dragged unwillingly to the chair by other MPs. This custom dates back to the speaker's original function of communicating the opinion of the Commons to the monarch, potentially facing the monarch's anger and subsequent retribution (death)

- When voting in the Commons, MPs say 'aye' or 'no'. Lord members vote saying 'content' or 'not content'

Both of the houses have maces – silver-gilt ornamental clubs – that symbolize the royal authority by which Parliament meets and the authority of the speaker. They are carried before the speakers of both Houses when they enter or leave the chamber. Interfering with the mace is considered gross disorderly conduct. Several MPs have manhandled the mace, including Conservative MP Michael Heseltine who, having lost a vote to an amendment of a Bill in 1976, seized the mace and brandished it at the opposing Labour Party after some Welsh MPs had sung the Labour Party anthem, 'The Red Flag'. The next morning he apologized unreservedly. In 1987, Labour MP Ron Brown threw the mace to the floor, damaging it and, when he refused to apologize to the speaker, was suspended from the Commons and the Labour Party. Labour MP John McDonnell was similarly suspended from the Commons for five days in 2009 when he picked up the mace.

Whips

Whips are MPs or Lords (see page 158) appointed by each party to ensure discipline and attendance at voting time in the House of Commons. The word 'whip' derives from hunting terminology: the huntsman's assistant who drives straying hounds back to the main pack using a whip is known as a 'whipper-in'.

Prime Minister's Questions

Prime Minister's Questions is held for around half-an-hour every Wednesday in the House of Commons, during which time the prime minister answers questions from MPs. Exchanges between the PM and opposition members can frequently turn nasty and the onus is very much on the PM to exercise authority within the chamber. There are few, other than perhaps Margaret Thatcher, who actually enjoyed these political bouts.

THE HOUSE OF LORDS

'Five hundred men chosen at random from the ranks of
the unemployed.'

THEN CHANCELLOR AND LATER PM LLOYD GEORGE (1863–1945)
CASTS ASPERSIONS ON THE UNELECTED PEERS OF
THE HOUSE OF LORDS AS THEY ATTEMPT TO
BLOCK HIS REFORMING BUDGET OF 1909.

The House of Lords is made up of around 642 life peers
and peeresses (i.e. those who have been appointed by the
prime minister, other political parties and an independent
appointments commission), around ninety-two hereditary
peers and peeresses (elected by other hereditary peers),
the Archbishops of York and Canterbury and twenty-six
senior Church of England bishops.

Prior to 1958, all peers in the House of Lords were
hereditary peers, senior judges or bishops, and since 1999
hereditary peers (of which there were several hundred)
have lost the automatic right to attend the House of Lords.
Now only ninety-two hereditary peers, as elected by other
peers, can sit in the House of Lords (and only two are
currently women).

Demands are frequently made to replace the House
of Lords with elected representatives, although others
argue that this would threaten the power of the House of
Commons. Currently the House of Lords provides a less
partisan and more experienced forum of debate, checking
laws that have been passed by the House of Commons and

holding the government to account, as well as proposing or amending new laws which are then discussed by MPs.

Woolsack

The Lord Speaker in the House of Lords sits on the Woolsack, which is a large red cushion or seat originally stuffed with wool. Edward III (1312–77) introduced this custom as a reminder of the pre-eminence of the wool trade in England. The woolsack has now been re-stuffed with wool from nations across the Commonwealth as a symbol of unity.

Black Rod

Responsible for security and order within the House of Lords, Black Rod is best known for his role in the state opening of Parliament. Traditionally, Black Rod is sent from the House of Lords to the Commons, where the door is slammed in his face (to symbolize the independence of the lower chamber). He then bangs the door three times with his rod, the door opens and MPs follow Black Rod back to the House of Lords to hear the Queen's speech.

Now as much a tradition as the rest of the proceedings, Labour MP and republican Dennis Skinner remains in the House of Commons during the Queen's Speech and traditionally jokes to Black Rod upon his arrival into the House. Quips have ranged from 'Hey up, here comes Puss in Boots!' in 1988, and, in reference to the Queen, 'Tell her to pay her taxes' in 1992. The 'Beast of Bolsover', as he is nicknamed, has been suspended from the House on at least ten occasions, although he never misses a sitting of Parliament, stating, 'If you missed a shift at the pit, you would get the sack.'

WHO CAN STAND AS MP?

Citizens of the UK, Republic of Ireland and the Commonwealth can stand for public office. Those who can't include: members of the House of Lords, civil servants, members of the armed forces and people convicted of certain criminal offences.

THE COFFERS

The current annual salary for an MP is £67,060 and MPs also receive expenses to cover costs of travelling between Parliament and their constituency, employing staff, running an office and having a base in London.

Most members of the House of Lords do not receive a salary but are entitled to claim a daily allowance of £300 per sitting day.

TRUST IN MPS

'Politicians continue to have the lowest level of public trust, well below that of bankers. However, we have never trusted politicians much.'

BEN PAGE, CHIEF EXECUTIVE OF IPSOS MORI.

Public trust in politicians and government ministers has declined sharply over the past decade, following scandals over MPs' expenses and the bailout of the banks.

A nationwide Ipsos MORI (Market & Opinion Research International) poll conducted in 2011 revealed that politicians are still the least trusted profession, with just one in seven people (14 per cent) saying they trust politicians in general to tell the truth. Just one person in six (17 per cent) say they trust government ministers. The City and Fleet Street fared better in the poll, with 29 per cent saying they trust business leaders and 19 per cent trust journalists. The most trusted professionals are doctors, with almost 9 out of 10 (88 per cent) of adults saying they trust them to tell the truth.

The Expenses Scandal

'I paid for it myself and in fact it was never liked by the ducks.'

FORMER GOSPORT CONSERVATIVE MP PETER VIGGERS IN MAY 2009
ON HIS CLAIM FOR £1,645 FOR A FLOATING DUCK HOUSE,
A REQUEST THAT WAS REJECTED BY THE FEES OFFICE.
THE DUCK ISLAND (WHICH WAS LATER SOLD, THE PROCEEDS
OF WHICH WERE HANDED OVER TO CHARITY) BECAME A
SYMBOL OF THE EXPENSES SCANDAL.

MPs' claims for excessive and sometimes dubious expenses when in office, made public by the *Telegraph* newspaper in 2009, caused scandal and public outrage, contributing to the public's distrust of MPs and politics in general. The scandal resulted in a large number of resignations, sackings and prosecutions (to include members of the House of Lords) as well as repayment of expenses and public apologies.

> 'Perhaps we need not more people looking round more corners but the same people looking round more corners more thoroughly to avoid the small things detracting from the big things the Prime Minister is getting right.'

> LORD MANDELSON ON THE INVESTIGATIONS INTO MPS' EXPENSES IN 2009. THE COMMENT EARNED HIM THE 'FOOT IN MOUTH AWARD' AS PRESENTED TO HIM BY THE PLAIN ENGLISH CAMPAIGN, SET UP TO ROOT OUT GOBBLEDEGOOK AND JARGON IN GOVERNMENTAL DEPARTMENTS AND PUBLIC LIFE (SEE PAGE 243).

BEYOND PARLIAMENT

The Houses of Parliament are not the only hotbeds of political action. Here we look at life beyond Westminster.

THE CIVIL SERVICE

'Give a civil servant a good case and he'll wreck it
with clichés, bad punctuation, double negatives and
convoluted apology.'

CONSERVATIVE POLITICIAN ALAN CLARK (1928–99)
IN HIS DIARY, 22 JULY 1983.

The Civil Service implements government policy and delivers public services. Servants are responsible to the minister of their department, and expected to be politically neutral, working for whichever party is in power. There are around 500,000 civil servants working in central London and around Britain, with 23 per cent of the entire service working for the Department of Work and Pensions, 15.9 per cent for HM Revenue & Customs, 15.9 per cent for the Ministry of Justice and 15.3 per cent for the Ministry of Defence.

The service is frequently criticized over its inefficiency and cost-effectiveness, the stereotypical image being that it is plagued by bureaucracy and that there is a 'Civil Service' way of doing things. The Civil Service's core values, as outlined in an official code of standard behaviour, are integrity, honesty, objectivity and impartiality – values and standards of behaviour that it expects all civil servants to uphold.

THE VOTING SYSTEM

Young people can vote in the UK from the age of eighteen. First-time voters, however, tend not to be interested in the political process, with only an estimated 43 per cent of registered young people aged 18–24 voting in the 2015 UK general election.

British, Commonwealth and Irish Republican citizens can vote in a general election if they are resident in the UK, aged eighteen and over, and not subject to any disqualification. Adult citizens not permitted to vote include:

- Convicted prisoners (although remand prisoners, un-convicted prisoners, and civil prisoners who are on the electoral register can vote)

- Members of the House of Lords (although they can vote in local authority elections, devolved legislatures and the European Parliament)

- EU citizens resident in the UK (although they can vote in local, devolved and European Parliament elections)

- Mentally ill patients detained compulsorily in prison or hospital and sufferers of severe mental illness who cannot understand the political system

The turnout of voters for a general election is typically around 70 per cent of the electorate, although this proportion has been declining in recent years. In 2015, the electorate turnout was 66 per cent, 65.4 per cent in

2005 and a low of 59.5 per cent in 2001. The highest electoral turnout since 1945 was in 1950 at 83.9 per cent. Currently, MPs are voted through the 'first past the post system', which means the candidate that wins the most votes in a constituency is elected MP for that area.

WHAT ARE QUANGOS?

Quango stands for Quasi-Autonomous Non-Governmental Organization. They are organizations that are funded by taxpayers but are not part of the civil service or controlled directly by central government. They can range from tiny committees to organizations with multi-million-pound budgets, and they can deliver public services, give advice or regulate behaviour. Organizations include the Environment Agency, the Sports Council, the Arts Council, the Crown Prosecution Service, the Equality and Human Rights Commission, and national galleries and museums. In 2010, the Cabinet Office list for 'non-departmental public bodies' totalled 742 across the UK, with the decision taken to abolish 192 and merge 118 bodies that same year in a bid to reduce the budget deficit.

LOCAL GOVERNMENT

Local authorities, or democratically elected councils, govern towns, cities and rural areas in the UK. Large towns and cities tend to be administered by a single local authority, while other areas have both district and county councils. Local authorities provide a range of services, from fire services, education and social services to housing, libraries and rubbish collection. Parish, community and town councils are elected and operate at a level below district councils and help with local issues such as neighbourhood planning, community centres and play areas.

Approximately 20 per cent of money for local authority services is funded by the collection of council tax, the rest comes from central government. Elections for local government councillors are held in May each year, and many candidates stand as members of a political party. A few local authorities appoint a mayor, who is the ceremonial leader of the council, and in some towns and cities a mayor is elected to be the leader of the administration. In 2013, there were sixteen directly elected mayors in England, including the Mayor of London.

Since July 2000, London has been run by a devolved Greater London Authority, with an elected mayor and London Assembly made up of twenty-five members responsible for the strategic government of Greater London (including the City of London). The role of Mayor of London was the first directly elected mayor in the UK.

There is also a Lord Mayor of the City of London, but this role is largely ceremonial and refers to the much smaller region of the City of London.

BORIS

'Look the point is ... Er, what is the point? It is a tough job but somebody has got to do it.'

ON BEING APPOINTED SHADOW ARTS MINISTER, THE *DAILY TELEGRAPH*, 7 MAY 2004.

Conservative MP and ex-journalist Boris Johnson was elected Mayor of London on 4 May 2008, defeating the previous Labour incumbent Ken Livingstone. He did so again in 2012. Often identified by his first name alone, Boris is one of the most recognized and popular figures in British politics, known for his outspokenness (which has frequently got him into trouble), eccentric but Establishment image and unruly mop of blond hair. Past gaffes include describing Portsmouth as 'too full of drugs, obesity, underachievement and Labour MPs'.

'The excitement is growing so much I think the Geiger counter of Olympomania is going to go zoink off the scale.'

ON THE FORTHCOMING LONDON OLYMPIC GAMES, THE *DAILY TELEGRAPH*, 27 JULY 2012.

DEVOLVED GOVERNMENT

Since 1999 there has been an elected Parliament in Scotland and an Assembly in Wales, and in 1998 Northern Ireland achieved an elected Assembly with significant legislative and executive authority.

THE NORTHERN IRELAND ASSEMBLY

The partition of Ireland in 1921–22 into the Irish Free State (later the Republic of Ireland, see page 63) and Northern Ireland led to the establishment of a devolved Parliament in Northern Ireland at Stormont (often used as the name for Parliament) in Belfast. Following the outbreak of the Troubles in 1968, it was suspended in 1972. Years of violence (over 3,600 people were killed) and distrust followed until a negotiated ceasefire by the main paramilitary groups, the IRA (Irish Republican Army) and the UDA (Ulster Defence Association), led to the Belfast Agreement (or Good Friday Agreement) in 1998.

Shortly afterwards, the Northern Ireland Assembly was set up based on a power-sharing agreement that distributes ministerial offices among the main parties. The Assembly has 108 elected members, known as MLAs (Members of the Legislative Assembly) elected by proportional representation (see opposite), and it can make decisions on all matters except those reserved for Westminster (defence, foreign policy and raising taxes). The UK government, however, has the power to suspend the Assembly, which it did in 2000, 2001 and 2002 until May 2007, largely because of the failure of the IRA to disarm until 2005. The Assembly was restored in 2007, with some previously reserved UK powers over prisons and criminal justice, security and policing transferred from Westminster in 2010.

IN PROPORTION

Proportional representation covers a wide variety of electoral systems whereby seats in Parliament are roughly in proportion to the number of votes cast. Forms of proportional representation are used for elections in Wales, Scotland and Northern Ireland as well as the London mayoral election, and throughout Europe.

THE SCOTTISH PARLIAMENT

'Nobody ever celebrated Devolution Day.'

MP FOR GORDON, ALEX SALMOND, UPHOLDS
HIS BELIEF IN FULL SCOTTISH INDEPENDENCE,
IN THE *INDEPENDENT*, 2 APRIL 1992.

Demand for more independence and democratic control in Scotland grew throughout the 1980s and 1990s. A Scottish devolution referendum in 1997 finally led to the establishment in 1999 of a new devolved Scottish Parliament in the Holyrood area of Edinburgh.

There are 129 members of the Scottish Parliament (MSPs) who are elected by a form of proportional representation. The Scottish Parliament has legislative powers, passing laws on anything not specifically reserved for Westminster (defence, social security, foreign affairs and general economic policies). It also has tax-varying powers, with the authority to make small changes to the lower base rate of income tax (known as the 'Tartan Tax'). The programmes of legislation enacted by the Scottish Parliament have seen a divergence in public services: unlike the rest of the UK, university education and care services for the elderly are free in Scotland. The Scottish Parliament currently has a majority Scottish National Party, with Nicola Sturgeon as the current First Minister of Scotland. In May 2012, under the leadership of Alex Salmond, the Scottish National Party launched a campaign for full Scottish independence. In the referendum held on 18 September 2014, 55 per cent of the country voted against independence from the UK.

THE NATIONAL ASSEMBLY FOR WALES

Based in Cardiff, the National Assembly for Wales was created in 1998 following a referendum the previous year in which the people of Wales voted for devolution by the thinnest of margins (50.3 per cent to 49.7 per cent). It comprises sixty members, known as Assembly Members (AMs), and elections are held every four years by a form of proportional representation. Prior to 1997, the Assembly had no primary legislative or fiscal powers, although it now has the power to make laws in twenty areas, to include education and training, housing, health and social services, and environment, and it can influence the rate of council tax set by local authorities. Notable differences in government services include the abolition of charges for NHS prescriptions (charges apply elsewhere in the UK).

THE EUROPEAN UNION

'We are with Europe, but not of it. We are linked but not comprised. We are interested and associated but not absorbed.'

WINSTON CHURCHILL IN THE *SATURDAY EVENING POST*, FEBRUARY 1930.

The idea of a united Europe originated in the period after the Second World War, as a means to create a prosperous Europe and to reduce the likelihood of another European War. In 1957, West Germany, France, Belgium, the Netherlands, Luxembourg and Italy signed the Treaty of Rome, forming the European Economic Community (EEC). Britain did not want to join then as it saw its future in trading with the Commonwealth and fostering its special relationship with the US. In 1973, after twice being vetoed by the French, the UK joined the EEC. In 2004, ten new member countries joined what was now called the European Union bringing membership to twenty-five.

The Maastricht Treaty in 1992 created the European Union and provided for the introduction of a common European currency, the euro, a European bank and common defence, foreign and social policies. In 2009, the Lisbon Treaty came into force, reforming many areas of the EU, to include creating a permanent president of the European Council.

There are currently twenty-eight member states in the European Union and one of its main aims is to create a single market so that goods, people and services can move freely between each. In 1993, a single market was established and in 1999 a monetary union, the eurozone, was established with eleven initial member states. Britain did not join the euro – its policy was to wait and see how the currency developed and put it to a referendum. In 2011, the population of the EU represented 7.3 per cent of the world population and generated a 20 per cent share of the global imports and exports.

Citizens of the European Union have the right to travel to any EU country so long as they have a valid identity card or passport. European Union citizens also have the right to work in any member state country.

European law is legally binding in all member states of the Union, including the UK, and is usually called directives, regulations or framework decisions. EU laws can range from limits on the hours that drivers of goods vehicles can work to the 2011 directive that all herbal medicine products must be licensed or prescribed by a registered herbal practitioner.

THE COUNCIL OF EUROPE

The Council of Europe was created in 1949, with the UK as one of its founder members. With forty-seven member countries, it works to protect human rights in those countries, and is separate from the EU (although, rather confusingly, it shares the same flag and anthem as the EU and is also based, like the European Parliament, in Strasbourg). Unlike the EU, the Council of Europe cannot make binding laws but draws up conventions and charters, the most well known being the European Convention on Human Rights and Fundamental Freedoms. The UK was one of the first countries to sign up to the convention and its principles include: freedom of thought, conscience and religion, freedom of expression (speech), the right to a fair trial, the right to life, the prohibition of torture, slavery and forced labour.

THE EUROPEAN PARLIAMENT

The European Parliament represents the 500 million citizens of the European Union and meets in Strasbourg in north-eastern France, and Brussels in Belgium. The parliament is headed by a president, who is elected by the MEPs who comprise it. Out of a total of 751 MEPs, seventy-five are from the UK, with each country electing members roughly in proportion to its population. Elections for MEPs are held every five years and an MEP cannot also be a member of a national parliament. Much of the detailed work of the parliament is undertaken by twenty permanent committees, such as foreign affairs and civil liberties.

THE EUROPEAN COMMISSION

The European Commission is the executive body of the European Union and it is made up of one representative (known as a commissioner) from each member state. (Commissioners are required to leave their national allegiances behind and 'think European'.) Primarily based in Brussels, the EC proposes legislation, and it is the job of the parliament and Council of Ministers to decide whether the law should take effect. The EC also proposes the annual budget of the European Union, which the European Parliament approves.

THE COUNCIL OF THE EUROPEAN UNION

The Council of Ministers, also based in Brussels, is another European organization permitted to pass laws. Whereas the European Parliament is meant to represent the citizens of Europe, the Council of Ministers represents national governments. It is made up of a relevant government minister from each member state, and it has powers to discuss and vote on the more intergovernmental matters of the EU, such as foreign policy.

'Whereas in England all is permitted that is not expressly prohibited, it has been said that in Germany all is prohibited unless expressly permitted, and in France all is permitted that is expressly prohibited. In the European Common Market [as it then was] no one knows what is permitted and it all costs more.'

ROBERT MEGARRY (1910–2006), ENGLISH JUDGE
IN A LECTURE DELIVERED ON 22 MARCH 1972.

THE EUROPEAN COUNCIL

Not to be confused with the Council of Ministers, the European Council is a meeting of all heads of government of the EU member states held twice every six months. It looks at the broad policies of the EU and its future direction. In 2014 the Council appointed Donald Tusk as president.

'TO BE OR NOT TO BE?'

'In my lifetime all our problems have come from mainland Europe and all the solutions have come from the English-speaking nations across the world.'

MARGARET THATCHER (1925–2013) IN *THE TIMES*,
6 OCTOBER 1999.

Margaret Thatcher supported British membership of the EEC, but felt that the European Union should be limited to free trade. She was also opposed to the increased centralization of decision-making in Europe and to monetary union. In 1990, she warned of the dangers of a single currency that could not accommodate industrial powerhouses like Germany as well as small countries like Greece, and that the euro would prove fatal to the poor countries because it would 'devastate their insufficient economies'.

British membership of the EU has always had its detractors in the UK with Euro-sceptics arguing that Britain's independence and sovereignty are threatened by European Union developments. The British public tend to have a negative impression of the European Union and traditionally list it well below other issues like the economy, pensions, crime, immigration and health. The turnout for the British EU Parliament elections is the lowest in Europe: in 2014, the average turnout in Europe was 43 per cent, in the UK it was 35.4 per cent.

The recent economic turmoil and debt crisis in the eurozone has led to increased pressure on the prime minister from his own party to call an immediate referendum on the EU. The right-wing Euro-sceptic UK Independence Party continues to grow in support (although they currently only have one seat in the House of Commons). In January 2013, David Cameron promised to hold an in–out referendum on Europe and a renegotiation of Britain's relationship with the EU, which will take place by the end of 2017.

THE UNITED NATIONS

The UK is part of the United Nations (UN), along with over 190 member countries. Based in New York, the UN was set up in 1945 after the Second World War to ensure peace, security and co-operation among the nations of the world. Britain is a permanent member of the UN Security Council, which serves to recommend action in the event of international crisis and threat to peace.

THE COMMONWEALTH

The Commonwealth is an association of countries, most of which were once part of the British Empire. The Queen is the ceremonial head of the Commonwealth and it currently has a membership of fifty-three states, amounting to 30 per cent of the world's population. Membership is voluntary and the Commonwealth has no formal constitution or by-laws. Member states consult and work together within a framework of common values and goals, to include the development of democracy, good government, human rights, gender equality, free trade and the eradication of poverty. Commonwealth nations also share strong trade links and Britain has huge overseas investments in the Commonwealth. A Commonwealth Heads of Government Meeting is held every two years.

NATO

The North Atlantic Treaty Organization is a political and military alliance between a group of European and North American countries. Member states, which currently number twenty-eight, agree to help each other in the event of an attack. Its headquarters are in Brussels.

'O JUST BUT SEVERE LAW!': THE UK LEGAL SYSTEM

Laws in the UK can be divided into criminal law and civil law.

CRIMINAL LAW

Criminal law relates to offences that are often investigated by the police. Those who violate the law in this way can be punished by the courts.

'I went out to Charing Cross, to see Major-general Harrison hanged, drawn, and quartered; which was done there, he looking as cheerful as any man could do in that condition.'

FROM THE *DIARY OF SAMUEL PEPYS*, 13 OCTOBER 1660.

MAGISTRATES' COURT

There are two levels of criminal courts: magistrates' courts and Crown courts. Magistrates' courts deal with less serious cases and 95 per cent of all criminal matters. Cases include motoring offences, burglary, minor criminal damage and matters that can be punished with community sentences, fines and short custodial sentences. There are over 360 magistrates' courts in England and Wales and most cases are heard by a bench of three lay magistrates (JPs) – part-time judicial officials chosen from the general community – who listen to cases without a jury and receive no salary for their work. More serious cases, often in larger cities, are presided over by district judges who are qualified lawyers.

CROWN COURT

Serious offences, like rape and murder, are tried by the Crown Court. They are situated in around seventy-eight cities in England and Wales, and are administered by the Ministry of Justice. The majority of cases are heard by a jury of twelve citizens, with sentences passed by a judge who is in charge of all proceedings in the court. Judges in Britain are senior lawyers appointed by the Lord Chancellor (who also fulfills the role of Secretary of State for Justice) from recommendations by the independent Judicial Appointments Commission. Judges (who are called 'the judiciary') ensure that trials are conducted fairly and are responsible for interpreting the law.

THE OLD BAILEY

The Central Criminal Court in London is commonly known as the Old Bailey after the street on which it is located. A bronze statue of Lady Justice, holding a sword in her right hand with the scales of justice in her left, stands on top of the dome above the central court.

THE SUPREME COURT

The highest court in England and Wales (and, in some cases, Northern Ireland and Scotland) is the Supreme Court in London. It is the final court of appeal in the UK and cannot consider a case unless a relevant order has been made in a lower court. For example, appeals against conviction in a Crown court can be referred to the Supreme Court as a final right of appeal. The Supreme Court also has jurisdiction to resolve disputes in relation to civil law and laws made by devolved governments in the UK. The court consists of twelve permanent Justices of the Supreme Court.

I FOUGHT THE LAW

The UK is home to a range of laws, including:

- It is a criminal offence to carry a weapon (to include a gun, a knife or anything that can cause injury) even if it is for self-defence

- The age of criminal responsibility in England and Wales is ten years old. Children are dealt with by youth courts and sent to special secure centres

- If you are under eighteen, it is against the law for you to buy alcohol or drink alcohol in licensed premises. However, if you are sixteen or seventeen and with an adult you can drink (but not buy) beer, wine or cider with a meal

- It is against the law to discriminate against anyone because of age, race (including colour, nationality, ethnic or national origin), religion, sex, sexual orientation, marriage status, gender reassignment, philosophical beliefs or maternity. This protection applies at work, in education, as a consumer, when using public services, buying or renting property and as a member or guest of a private club

- It is against the law to smoke tobacco products in most enclosed public spaces – a sign will usually indicate where it is not allowed

BEYOND THE BORDERS

Northern Ireland also has lower magistrates' courts and Crown courts. In Scotland, less serious criminal cases are tried by lay justices of the peace in district courts, while more serious offences are held in sheriffs courts, where a sheriff sits alongside a jury of fifteen. The High Court of Justiciary is the supreme criminal court in Scotland and a court of appeal, with cases heard by a judge and a jury of fifteen people.

CRIME FACTS

In 2009, there were 4.5 million crimes recorded in England and Wales. The survey by the Offending, Crime and Justice Survey shows that 10 per cent of offenders are responsible for 60 per cent of offences, and that serious and prolific offenders amount to 1 per cent of the population.

One in fifty crimes results in conviction and 50 per cent of victims do not report incidents to the police.

CIVIL LAW

Civil law deals with disputes between individuals and organizations, in which financial damages can be awarded to the losing party. Examples of civil law include disputes between landlords and tenants, employees and their employers, and matters relating to debt.

COUNTY COURTS

In England and Wales, 90 per cent of civil cases are dealt with in county courts, and the rest in the High Court. County courts (which are often referred to as small claims courts) handle cases for a range of matters, from divorce and families to property, contract and money. There are 250 county courts in England and Wales, and each case is presided over by a district judge.

THE HIGH COURT OF JUSTICE

The High Court of Justice deals with more complex cases; its main centre is in London with branches throughout England and Wales. However, most civil disputes are resolved by tribunals and don't reach the court system. In Northern Ireland, the Northern Irish High Court deals with most civil cases, as does the sheriff court in Scotland.

YOUNG OFFENDERS

Young offenders are a major problem in the UK – 10 per cent of criminal offences are committed by young persons under the age of sixteen, and the peak age for committing crime is fifteen.

In England, Wales and Northern Ireland, young people aged between ten and seventeen who have been accused of an offence have their cases heard in a youth court, which is presided over by a district judge or by specially trained magistrates. In Scotland, the Children's Hearings System deals with the cases of young people.

ASBOs or Anti-Social Behaviour Orders are a recent attempt to control social disorder and anyone over the age of ten can be given an ASBO if they behave anti-socially (which includes drunken or threatening behaviour, vandalism or playing loud music). Penalties for offenders can include being banned from particular places or from drinking in the street etc.

LEGAL AID

Legal aid, in the form of payment by the state for legal advice or representation, was first brought into effect in Britain in 1949. In Scotland, legal aid does not cover representation at tribunals or small claims in the sheriff court. In Northern Ireland, civil legal aid is subject to a financial eligibility test and criminal legal aid is subject to a means and merits test. As of April 2013, major changes have been made to civil legal aid. Certain cases (except in very limited circumstances) will no longer be eligible, including divorce and immigration.

STRANGE BUT TRUE

The following laws are allegedly still in existence in the statute book in England and Wales:

- It is illegal to enter the Houses of Parliament wearing a suit of armour
- It is illegal to eat mince pies on Christmas Day
- It could be regarded as an act of treason to place a postage stamp bearing the Queen's image upside down
- A pregnant woman can legally relieve herself in public
- The head of any dead whale found on the British coast becomes the property of the king and the tail the queen

THE DEATH PENALTY

The death penalty was formally abolished in Britain in 1965 and in Northern Ireland in 1973. The last executions in the UK took place in 1964. In September 2010, YouGov conducted an opinion poll asking people directly if they wanted the death penalty reinstated – 51 per cent said 'yes'.

'IN SWEET MUSIC IS SUCH ART': CULTURE

From Elgar to jellied eels, afternoon tea to pantomimes, British culture is nothing if not varied. For all budding culture vultures, this chapter is dedicated to the country's rich heritage, past and present.

PUBLIC HOLIDAYS, FESTIVALS AND TRADITIONS

New Year's Day, 1 January A public holiday throughout the UK. The evening before (New Year's Eve) is celebrated with fireworks and parties. In Scotland, New Year's Eve (known as Hogmanay) is celebrated with an array of customs, including 'First Footing', when the first person (preferably a tall, dark man) to cross the threshold of a house immediately after midnight gives a gift like coal to bring luck for the rest of the year.

DAYS GONE BY

The lyrics to the song 'Auld Lang Syne' come from a poem written by Robert Burns in 1788 and are set to a traditional folk melody. Traditionally sung by people with linked crossed arms as the clock strikes midnight for New Year's Day, 'Auld Lang Syne' can be translated as 'Days gone by', and is usually interpreted as a call to remember long-standing friendships.

In 2000, the Queen was berated by the press for not crossing hands with Tony Blair while singing 'Auld Lang Syne' at the Millennium Dome celebrations. In fact, she was correctly following the Scottish tradition of not crossing hands until the last verse.

St Valentine's Day, 14 February While not a public holiday in the UK, 14 February has been observed each year throughout the UK as a celebration of romantic love. Its origin is subject to conjecture, although the first official Saint Valentine's Day was declared by Pope Gelasius in 496 in memory of a third-century priest in Rome (who, legend tells us, performed secret marriages for Roman soldiers for whom marriage was forbidden).

St David's Day, 1 March   Commemorates the death of the patron saint of Wales (see page 29). In 2007, the National Assembly for Wales voted unanimously to make St David's Day a bank holiday (as backed by 87 per cent of Welsh people) but this was rejected by the then prime minister Tony Blair.

Mothering Sunday, the fourth Sunday of Lent
A day to celebrate and give thanks to mothers.

St Patrick's Day, 17 March   The anniversary of the death of St Patrick, the patron saint of Ireland (see page 31). A public holiday in Northern Ireland and the Republic of Ireland, St Patrick's Day sees people wearing green and donning shamrocks in the saint's honour (St Patrick is said to have used the shamrock, a three-leaved plant, to explain the Holy Trinity to his followers).

Easter, the first Sunday after the first full moon on or after 21 March   Easter is a Christian festival that encompasses two public holidays, one on Good Friday and the Monday after Easter Sunday. Good Friday marks the death of Jesus Christ and Easter Sunday his rising. Eggs are given at Easter as a symbol of new life and springtime: originally these were painted birds' eggs, but are now, more commonly, chocolate eggs.

189

LENT

According to the Christian calendar, Lent is the period of forty days before Easter. Christians replicate Jesus Christ's withdrawal into the desert for forty days by fasting from food and festivities. Shrove Tuesday (also known as Pancake Day) is the last day before Lent and pancakes are eaten on this day because they used up all the eggs, fats and milk in the house, with just the addition of flour; foods that wouldn't last the forty days of Lent.

April Fool's Day, 1 April Although not a national holiday, fun is had for the first half of the day, at least, when people play practical jokes on each other until the clock strikes midday.

The media often runs spoof stories on this day, such as: 'The Government is planning to mitigate the damage caused by adding VAT to pasties by introducing a new "green" tax on chilled champagne.' A spoof report in the *Mail on Sunday* on 1 April 2012.

Vaisakhi (also known as Bisakhi), 13 or 14 April A Sikh New Year festival, it also commemorates 1699, the year Sikhism was born as a collective faith. Parades, dancing and singing are performed throughout the day.

St George's Day, 23 April   Not a national holiday, St George's Day remembers the death of the English patron saint in AD 303 (see page 29). Traditional celebrations have waned in England over the past few decades, although organizations such as English Heritage and the Mayor of London Boris Johnson have been encouraging its celebration, and Conservative MP Andrew Rosindell has advocated that it be made a public holiday. Many English people (as many as one-quarter) are unaware that St George is the patron saint of England, and there have been some calls for him to be replaced by another, less obscure patron saint.

Father's Day, the third Sunday in June   A day to honour fathers, it originated in the US in the twentieth century and is not a public holiday in the UK.

Diwali, mid-October to mid-November   Popularly known as the 'festival of lights', this five-day festival is celebrated by Hindus and Sikhs in honour of the inner light and higher knowledge. All celebrants wear new clothes, share sweets and snacks, and keep lamps burning overnight to signify the triumph of good over evil.

Halloween, 31 October   A contraction of All Hallows' Evening, Halloween is the eve of the Christian feast of All Hallows (or All Saints). Its origins are obscure but it is linked to an ancient pagan festival to mark the beginning of winter. In the evening, children dress up in a variety of

191

scary costumes and go out 'trick or treating' as well as carving pumpkins into lanterns.

Hanukkah, November or December The Jewish Festival of lights, Hannukah remembers the Jewish struggle for religious freedom and rededication of the Holy Temple in Jerusalem in the second century BC. It is celebrated by lighting one candle on the hanukiah or menorah (an eight-stemmed candelabrum) each day.

Eid al-Fitr Muslims celebrate the end of Ramadan, the Islamic holy month of fasting, on the day of Eid, thanking Allah for giving them the strength throughout the previous month. Celebrated at different times every year, Eid is commemorated with special services and a celebratory meal.

Eid ul-Adha A Muslim festival that remembers the prophet Ibrahim's willingness to sacrifice his son upon God's orders. During the festival some Muslims sacrifice domestic animals (British law stipulates this must be done in a slaughterhouse), and festivities also include prayers and presents. It is celebrated at different times of the year.

Bonfire Night, 5 November Also known as Guy Fawkes Night, Bonfire Night remembers Guy Fawkes' foiled attempt to blow up the Houses of Parliament in 1605 (see page 49).

Remembrance Day, 11 a.m. on the second Sunday of November   At this time people across the UK hold a two-minute silence to remember those who have died in conflicts since the First World War. The Queen also lays a wreath at the Cenotaph, the United Kingdom's official war memorial in Whitehall, London. A two-minute silence is additionally held at 11 a.m. on 11 November to commemorate the end of the First World War at 11 a.m. on the eleventh day of the eleventh month in 1918. People honour the war dead by wearing a poppy because these flowers grew on the battlefields after the First World War.

St Andrew's Day, 30 November   In 2006, the Scottish Parliament designated St Andrew's Day, the feast day of the patron saint of Scotland, a public holiday. All things Scottish are also celebrated on the day, with the flying of the saltire flag, bagpipe music and dancing.

Christmas Day and Boxing Day, 25 and 26 December respectively   Both days are public holidays in the United Kingdom. Christmas Day commemorates the birth of Jesus Christ and Boxing Day was traditionally a day when servants would receive gifts from their masters. Christmas is celebrated with feasting, the exchange of gifts and carol singing.

BANK HOLIDAYS

Along with holidays and festivities, the UK has a number of public holidays, known as bank holidays, when banks and many businesses are closed. Bank holidays include the first and last Mondays of May, 12 July in Northern Ireland, in remembrance of the Battle of the Boyne (celebrating the Glorious Revolution in 1688, see page 51) and the last Monday of August in England, Wales and Northern Ireland.

IT'S OFFICIAL

Bank holidays were once dubbed 'St Lubbock's Days' in honour of the nineteenth-century Liberal MP and banker Sir John Lubbock, who succeeded in bringing in legislation in 1871 that specified the UK's bank holidays (including, for the first time, the August bank holiday). He ensured that banks were closed on such days, as this would ensure that employers of all businesses would follow suit. Until then, the only national holidays in the UK were on Good Friday and Christmas Day.

May Day, held on 1 May, is an ancient festival in the UK (celebrated by the Celts and Romans) in celebration of the coming of summer, with a host of merriment involving maypoles and morris dancers. In 1978, Labour prime minister James Callaghan (1912–2005) created a bank holiday on the first Monday in May in recognition of the socialist workers' movement and International Workers' Day, and the Conservatives have wanted to eradicate it ever since. In 2011, the UK's coalition government drew up plans to cancel the May Day bank holiday and replace it with a Trafalgar Day in October, or a St George's Day in April in England or a St David's Day in March in Wales.

LEISURE AND PASTIMES

The British certainly know how to fill their spare time, as the following entries show.

GARDENING

A favourite British pastime on a public holiday is to potter in the garden. The British love to garden whether it's in their own backyard, patio or garden in hanging baskets and window boxes or on a rented parcel of land known as allotments (see page 196). There are numerous gardening television and radio programmes and every May crowds flock to the Chelsea Flower Show in London.

GROW YOUR OWN

The popularity of the allotment in the UK has risen and fallen in inverse proportion to the nation's well-being. During the Second World War's 'Dig for Victory' campaign, there were some 1,300,000 allotments in Britain. The strikes and energy shortages in the 1970s, along with the TV sitcom *The Good Life* (in which a husband and wife attempt to live a sustainable lifestyle), encouraged people to start growing their own food in allotments. The recent credit crunch has seen an upsurge in popularity for self-sufficiency, although numbers are still low compared to earlier years with an estimated 250,000 allotments in 2009.

COUNTRYSIDE AND WALKING

The British passion for plants and the countryside is also reflected in the popular pursuits of walking, rambling and hiking. Some 865,000 hectares of mountain, heathland, downland and moorland can be accessed by the public and 118,000 miles (190,000 km) of public rights of way criss-cross private land in the UK. Anyone can use a public right of way at any time, and there are scores of organizations dedicated to the preservation of right of access.

Public rights of way are usually accompanied by signs and symbols: a yellow arrow indicates a public footpath open to walkers only and a blue arrow indicates a bridleway, which are open to walkers, cyclists and horse-riders. An acorn identifies one of fifteen long-distance routes in England and Wales, which provide outstanding walking, cycling and horse-riding routes.

Foot-and-Mouth Disease

'The report speaks for itself. It's a very good report. It's a very long report. I haven't read the report.'

KEITH VAZ, LABOUR MP, ON THE REPORT OF THE COMMITTEE OF INQUIRY INTO THE OUTBREAK OF FOOT-AND-MOUTH DISEASE IN BRITAIN, 2001.

The outbreak of foot-and-mouth disease, an infectious disease affecting farm animals, in 2001 (the last outbreak had been in 1967) led to the closure of public rights of way – decimating tourism in the worst affected areas (Cumbria, in particular) – and the slaughter of 10 million sheep and cattle.

HUNTING, SHOOTING AND FISHING

The tradition of hunting, shooting and fishing has long been a feature of country life in Britain, although these 'blood sports' have met considerable opposition on the grounds of cruelty to animals. Hunting usually refers to fox hunting on horseback and the shooting of game birds. In the UK, deer hunting is usually referred to as 'deer stalking'.

> 'The English country gentleman galloping after a fox –
> the unspeakable in full pursuit of the uneatable.'
> OSCAR WILDE IN *A WOMAN OF NO IMPORTANCE* (1893).

Fox hunting has always generated passionate debate. Its defenders argue that it fulfils a pest-control function as part of a time-honoured rural way of life, while its opponents argue it violates animal rights and perpetuates the pretensions of Britain's social past. It was banned in Scotland in 2002, in England and Wales in 2004 (legislation covered all hunting with dogs) but remains legal in Northern Ireland. Hunting on the British mainland now follows artificially laid trails (known as 'drag hunting') or follows strict controls. As of February 2013, the Master of Foxhounds Association claims there are 179 active hunts in the UK.

OVERRULED

The passing of the hunting legislation in England and Wales in 2004 was notable because it was implemented without the approval of the House of Lords (who had rejected it). In order to do this, the Commons used the Parliament Acts of 1911 and 1949, which had reduced the power of the House of Lords to veto legislation. The Parliament Acts are employed rarely – they have been used to pass legislation against the House of Lords on only seven occasions since 1911.

Shooting, in particular pheasants, is a popular sport in the UK and the British Association for Shooting and Conservation estimates that over 1 million people participate annually (including clay and target shooting). There are specific seasons when game shooters and deer stalkers are allowed to hunt: in England, Scotland and Wales, the shooting season for pheasants runs from 1 October to 1 February and in Northern Ireland it runs from 1 October to 31 January; in England, Wales and Ireland, the shooting season for red deer stags runs from 1 August to 30 April, and from 1 July to 20 October in Scotland.

It is an offence (except in certain circumstances) to possess a shotgun without a current shotgun certificate or temporary police permit. It is an offence to give or sell a shotgun to someone who is not authorized to possess it.

Angling is one of the largest sports in the country. There is a legal closed season for freshwater fishing (coarse fishing) in rivers and streams between March and mid-June in England and Wales, to allow the fish to breed. You can enjoy coarse fishing all year round in Northern Ireland and Scotland, although there are seasons for salmon and trout fishing. You can fish in the sea at any time and in many still waters. The closed season for salmon varies in different parts of the UK, and for brown trout the closed season is generally winter, although this varies by region. Anyone over the age of twelve needs a rod licence to fish for freshwater fish. You don't need a rod licence in Scotland, nor do you need one for sea fishing in UK or Irish waters.

A HELPING HAND

'Ghillie' is the Scottish term for a 'fishing guide'. It is derived from the old Gaelic for manservant.

PETS

Despite the British penchant for blood sports, its people are known to be animal lovers and many people keep pets. More than 50 per cent of British families own a pet, with an estimated 26 per cent of UK households owning cats and 31 per cent owning dogs. The RSPCA (Royal Society for the Prevention of Cruelty to Animals) is one of the UK's most popular charities, collecting some £28.5 million in legacies each year.

MAN'S BEST FRIEND

A survey conducted in the late 1990s found that 60 per cent of dog owners in the UK preferred the company of their dog to that of their spouse.

The authorities take the keeping of pets very seriously, too. It is an offence to cause unnecessary physical or mental suffering to an animal. In public places, owners must control their dogs, putting them on a lead when appropriate, and dogs must wear a collar with the name and address of the owner. Owners must also clear up any dog faeces.

CHIEF MOUSER TO THE CABINET OFFICE

The resident cat at the PM's residence, 10 Downing Street, is officially known as the Chief Mouser to the Cabinet Office. The first cat to have been bestowed this official title was the tabby cat Larry, who arrived in 2011. A Downing Street spokesman said the former stray was a 'good ratter'.

Another famous cat to live at Number Ten was Humphrey, who was adopted in 1989 during Margaret Thatcher's premiership after wandering in as a stray. He stayed on throughout the premiership of John Major but shortly after the arrival of Tony Blair, rumours had started circulating that his wife, Cherie, did not like cats. At this point the PM's press officer Alastair Campbell swung into action, arranging a photocall with Humphrey and Cherie in the garden of Number Ten. Nonetheless, Humphrey retired soon after, with Whitehall officials claiming he was suffering from a kidney problem.

Conservative MP Alan Clark, however, suspected foul play and demanded proof that he was still alive: 'Humphrey is now a missing person. Unless I hear from him or he makes a full public appearance, I suspect he has been shot while trying to escape.'

THE QUEEN'S CORGIS

Dogs are the favoured pets of the royal family. Queen Victoria's much-loved collie, Noble, was given his own gravestone at Balmoral, and King Edward VII's terrier, Caesar, was given the honour of walking behind the king's coffin in his funeral procession. Queen Elizabeth II dotes upon her corgis after her father, King George VI, brought home a corgi called Dookie in 1933. Elizabeth was given a corgi named Susan for her eighteenth birthday, from which her current corgis are descended. In 2012, three of her corgis, Monty, Willow and Holly, featured in a scene filmed for the London 2012 Olympic Games, greeting James Bond as he arrived at Buckingham Palace. Monty died later that year, as did Cider, a 'dorgi', a dashsund-corgi cross-breed, also owned by the Queen.

BRITISH ORGANIZATIONS, CLUBS AND SOCIETIES

The British do like to form clubs and organizations, many of which have been exported around the world.

THE RSPB

'Who runs the country? The Royal Society for the
Protection of Birds. Their members are behind every
hedge.'

JOHN BETJEMAN

The largest wildlife conservation charity in Europe, the
RSPB (The Royal Society for the Protection of Birds) has
over 1 million members, 195,000 of them youth members.
It was founded in 1889 by Emily Williamson as a protest
group against the wearing of exotic feathers in hats, which
was the fashion at the time. It advises the government
on policies of conservation and environmentalism and
maintains over 200 bird reserves in the UK.

According to the 2012 RSPB Big Garden Birdwatch,
the top fifteen birds spotted in British gardens are:
blackbirds, blue tits, chaffinches, coal tits, collared doves,
dunnocks, goldfinches, great tits, greenfinches, house
sparrows, long-tailed tits, magpies, robins, starlings and
wood pigeons.

In London, the most common bird is the feral pigeon,
the cousin of the wood pigeon. Many Londoners view
them as little more than rats with wings. Trafalgar Square
used to be famous for its pigeons until London Mayor Ken
Livingstone drove out the birds in 2003 by banning the
feeding of pigeons in the square. Hawks are now flown in
the square in a bid to deter the pigeons.

THE NATIONAL TRUST

One of the UK's largest membership and charitable organizations, as well as one of the largest landowners, the National Trust looks after places of historical interest in England, Wales and Northern Ireland. (Scotland has an independent National Trust for Scotland.) The Trust was founded in 1894 to protect open spaces and threatened buildings.

Its membership, from which the National Trust derives much of its income, has grown staggeringly from 226,200 in 1970 to 2 million in 1990, and over 3.7 million in 2013 (six times more members than all the main political parties put together). Its phenomenal success is a reflection of the British people's sense of history and fascination with great houses of the past, as well as a general increase in leisure time and a growing population of retired people who like nothing more than to wander round a National Trust property, followed by a cup of tea (the Trust serves a lot of tea – 3.5 million cups a year).

FREEMASONRY

The secret society of Freemasons evolved from a stonemason and cathedral builders' guild in the Middle Ages. Honorary members were accepted and the rites and trappings of chivalric brotherhoods and ancient religious sects taken on, with the first Grand Lodge founded in England in 1717. Members are required to be male and to believe in the existence of a Supreme Being and the immortality of the soul (although Freemasons state that their organization is not a religion). Freemasonry exists in various forms around the world (2 million members in the US) and around 400,000 members in Scotland, Ireland and England.

THE SCOUT MOVEMENT

An informal organization for young people with an emphasis on practical outdoor activities, such as camping, sports and woodcraft, the UK movement encompasses Beaver Scouts, Cub Scouts and Boy Scouts, and Rainbow Guides, Brownie Guides and Girl Guides, with Venture Scouts for senior members. The movement was founded by the retired army general Robert Baden-Powell who, inspired by his military service during the 1880s and 1890s in India and Africa, put together a training programme for young people, holding a camp on Brownsea Island in Poole, Dorset, in 1907 to try out his ideas. His subsequent book *Scouting for Boys* became the handbook for the movement, along with the motto, 'Be Prepared'. The movement grew in the UK, British Empire and around the world, and membership today stands at 41 million members worldwide in the Scouting and Guiding movement, and 1 million members in the UK.

THE SALVATION ARMY

The Salvation Army was founded in London in 1865 by former Methodist minister William Booth and his wife, Catherine Booth. An integral part of Protestant Christianity, the Salvation Army adopted a quasi-military command structure with uniforms, flags and ranks, preaching, converting and administering the three 'S's: 'soup, soap, and salvation' to 'down-and-outs'. Its objectives are 'the advancement of the Christian religion ... of education, the relief of poverty, and other charitable objects beneficial to society or the community of mankind as a whole'. The movement now operates in 126 countries around the world, is one of the world's largest providers of social aid, and has a worldwide membership of 1.4 million.

READING AND LITERATURE

Reading is still a popular leisure activity for people in Britain, with 60 per cent of the population reading books. A large variety of books are published in the UK – per capita, the United Kingdom is the largest publisher worldwide, with the ebook market rapidly increasing. A handsome 58 per cent of the population own a library card and in 2011–12 there were 11,411,561 active borrowers. However, borrowing figures have been steadily dropping over recent years, and the government has been forced to close public libraries (since April 2011, 157 have been closed or handed over to unpaid volunteers).

Between 2002 and 2012, James Patterson was the most borrowed author for adults and Jacqueline Wilson was the most borrowed children's author. *The Da Vinci Code* was the most borrowed adult fiction title in that decade, and Charles Dickens, Jane Austen and Shakespeare the most borrowed pre-twentieth-century authors.

The literary festival scene is also thriving in the UK, with over 160 festivals held every year. The biggest literary festivals include the Hay Festival, which is held in Herefordshire in May, the Edinburgh International Book Festival in August, and the Cheltenham Festival of Literature in Gloucestershire in October.

FIRST PRINTING

According to the *Guinness Book of Records*, *Harry Potter and the Deathly Hallows*, the seventh and final instalment in the series, had an initial print run of 12 million copies when it was published in 2007 – the biggest initial print run for a fiction book in history.

THEATRE

The theatre in the UK is vibrant and innovative, with a worldwide reputation. There are some 300 commercial theatres around the country, with a concentration in

London's West End (also known as 'Theatreland') offering a range of theatre from musicals to dramas and comedies. Most theatres in the West End are commercially run although some, including the National Theatre and the Royal Shakespeare Company, receive public funding from the Arts Council. Public subsidy in UK theatre is considerably less than in many other European countries.

Drama flourished in the UK, particularly in the sixteenth and seventeenth centuries with the emergence of William Shakespeare (see page 210), as well as Ben Jonson, John Webster and Christopher Marlowe. In the nineteenth century, the plays of the Irishmen George Bernard Shaw and Oscar Wilde graced the London stages, along with those of Norwegian Henrik Ibsen. Since then, famous British playwrights have included Noël Coward, David Hare, John Osborne, Terence Rattigan, Harold Pinter, Alan Ayckbourn, Alan Bennett and Tom Stoppard.

Musical theatre also has a strong tradition in the UK, with Gilbert and Sullivan's nineteenth-century comic operas *HMS Pinafore* (1878), *The Mikado* (1885) and *The Pirates of Penzance* (1879) still popular today. More recently, Andrew Lloyd Webber's musicals, including *Jesus Christ Superstar* (1970), *Cats* (1981) and *The Phantom of the Opera* (1986), have dominated the West End, many transferring to Broadway, leading the *New York Times* to refer to Lloyd Webber in 2001 as 'the most commercially successful composer in history'.

ENDURING LOVE

'Fourteen months I am going to give it.'

PETER SAUNDERS.

'It won't run that long, eight months perhaps.'

AGATHA CHRISTIE.

Agatha Christie describes a conversation in her auto-biography with producer Peter Saunders about her new murder mystery play, *The Mousetrap*. Having opened in the West End in 1952, the play is now the world's longest-running theatre show, celebrating its 25,000th UK performance on 18 November 2012.

WILLIAM SHAKESPEARE

'A politician is one that would circumvent God.'

WILLIAM SHAKESPEARE, *HAMLET* (1603).

William Shakespeare (1564–1616) is often regarded as the world's greatest playwright. During his lifetime he wrote at least 154 sonnets and thirty-seven plays, which generally fall into three categories: tragedies, comedies and histories.

Little is known about his life other than that he was born in Stratford-upon-Avon, the son of glovemaker John Shakespeare and Mary Arden, and brother to three younger brothers and two younger sisters. In 1582, he married Anne Hathaway, who was eight years his senior, and together they had a daughter, Susanna, in 1583 and twins Hamnet and Judith in 1585. Hamnet died when he was just eleven. By 1594, Shakespeare had joined a well-known acting group called the Lord Chamberlain's Men, presenting plays for Queen Elizabeth I and King James I. In approximately 1610 he retired from the theatre, returned to Stratford-upon-Avon, where he died on 23 April 1616.

POETRY

British poets have written some of the most enduring verse in Western culture, from the great Anglo-Saxon epic poem *Beowulf* (AD 608) and the works of Geoffrey Chaucer, the greatest English poet of the Middle Ages, to John Donne, Shakespeare, John Milton, John Dryden, Robert Burns, Sir Walter Scott, William Wordsworth, Percy Shelley, Lord Byron, John Keats, W. B. Yeats, Siegfried Sassoon, Rupert Brooke, Wilfred Owen, W. H. Auden, Louis MacNeice, T. S. Eliot, Dylan Thomas, John Betjeman, Ted Hughes, Philip Larkin, Carol Ann Duffy, Andrew Motion, Wendy Cope and Benjamin Zephaniah, to name but a few.

DESPERATE MEASURES

Politicians, including the ex-Chancellor of the Exchequer Alistair Darling, ex-PM Gordon Brown and former president of the European Commission José Manuel Barroso, are fond of the phrase 'exceptional times require exceptional measures', particularly in reference to the turmoil of the worldwide recession.

In fact, variations of the phrase (the word 'exceptional' preferred by those in the political and legal fields) go back centuries: 'Diseases desperate grown, by desperate alliances are relieved, or not at all' is uttered by Shakespeare's *Hamlet*; Guy Fawkes, the man who tried to blow up Parliament (see page 49), is famed for saying 'Desperate diseases require desperate measures' after being questioned by the king and his council in 1605.

In 2009, the BBC launched an online vote to find the Nation's Favourite Poet. T. S. Eliot, author of 'The Love Song of J. Alfred Prufrock', 'The Waste Land' and 'Old Possum's Book of Practical Cats', was revealed as the winner. Other favourite poets (in descending order) were: John Donne, Benjamin Zephaniah, Wilfred Owen, Philip Larkin, William Blake, W. B. Yeats, John Betjeman, John Keats, and Dylan Thomas.

MUSIC

Britain has a rich musical heritage, from church music to classical, folk music to contemporary rock and pop, which sells around the world. Notable composers and musicians include:

Henry Purcell (1659–95) An English composer and organist at Westminster Abbey, Purcell wrote church music, operas (including *Dido and Aeneas* and *The Fairy-Queen*) and other pieces of Baroque music that were distinctly English in form.

Georg Friedrich Handel (1685–1759) A German-born composer, Handel settled in London in 1712 and became a British citizen in 1727. Regarded as one of the greatest composers of all time, he created over thirty operas, as well as numerous oratorios, organ concertos and anthems. His anthem 'Zadok the Priest' was written for the coronation ceremony of George II in 1727 and has been played at every British coronation ceremony since. The oratorio 'Messiah' is one of his best-known works.

Sir Edward Elgar (1857–1934) One of England's best-known composers, Elgar is known for the Enigma Variations and the Pomp and Circumstance Marches, of which 'March No.1' ('Land of Hope and Glory') usually begins the Last Night of the Proms (see page 214).

THE LAST NIGHT OF THE PROMS

Founded in 1895, the Proms is an eight-week season of classical music held at the Royal Albert Hall in London. The Last Night is typically exuberant and patriotic in tone, with 'prommers' waving Union flags. The concerts are officially known as the 'Henry Wood Promenade Concerts' after Sir Henry Wood (1869–1944), who conducted the Proms for nearly half a century.

Gustav Holst (1874–1934) An English composer with Nordic ancestry, Holst composed operas, ballets and choral hymns, with the orchestric suite 'The Planets' his most famous work.

Ralph Vaughan Williams (1872–1958) A celebrated English composer (whose ancestry includes Josiah Wedgewood and Charles Darwin), Williams' works include the orchestral piece 'The Lark Ascending'. Despite being dismissed as 'cow-pat music' by the composer Elisabeth Lutyens (1906–83), 'The Lark Ascending' has been consistently voted in polls as the nation's favourite piece of classical music.

Benjamin Britten (1913–76) A leading conductor, composer and pianist, Britten is best known for his operas *Billy Budd* and *Peter Grimes*. He also wrote music for children and founded the Aldeburgh Festival.

The Beatles A four-piece rock-and-roll band, the Beatles went on to become the most successful band in history, with sales of 1 billion units worldwide (according to EMI Records in 2001). The band was formed in 1960 and by 1962 had settled into its line-up of John Lennon, Paul McCartney, George Harrison and Ringo Starr. The Beatles' official UK LPs were *Please Please Me* (1963), *With the Beatles* (1963), *A Hard Day's Night* (1964), *Help!* (1965), *Rubber Soul* (1965), *Revolver* (1966), *Sgt Pepper's Lonely Hearts Club Band* (1967), *The Beatles* (1968), *Yellow Submarine* (1969), *Abbey Road* (1969) and *Let It Be* (1970).

FESTIVALS

There are a large number of music festivals in the UK. Glastonbury, held near Pilton in Somerset, is the world's biggest open-air arts and music festival. Farmer Michael Eavis held the first Glastonbury festival on 19 September 1970 (the day after Jimi Hendrix died), with acts including Marc Bolan and Keith Christmas and with an attendance of 1,500 – for the price of £1 (including free milk from Eavis's farm). In 2015, attendees numbered 135,000, tickets were priced at £220 and headline acts included Kanye West and The Who. Tickets frequently sell out in under two hours, with a new record set in 2015 of just 25 minutes. Headline acts have been varied, with artists such as the Rolling Stones, Beyonce, David Bowie and Stevie Wonder performing.

VISUAL ART

Britain has a strong tradition in landscape and watercolour, portraiture and caricature in the field of visual arts. Well-known British artists include Sir Joshua Reynolds (1723–92), who specialized in portrait painting, as did Scottish painter David Allan (1744–96); the English painter, printmaker and social satirist William Hogarth (1697–1764); J. M. W. Turner (1775–1850) and John Constable (1776–1837), who were both influential landscape painters (John Constable painted one of the best-known British paintings, 'The Hay Wain', in 1821 and Turner was the great master of watercolour landscape paintings); the great visionary poet and painter William Blake (1757–1827); the Pre-Raphaelites of the second half of the nineteenth century, which included John Everett Millais (1829–96) and Dante Gabriel Rossetti (1828–82), whose ideas influenced the Arts and Crafts designer William Morris (1834–96); Scottish designer and artist Charles Rennie Mackintosh (1868–1928), the main representative of Art Nouveau in Britain; leading English sculptors Henry Moore (1898–1986) and Barbara Hepworth (1903–75); figurative painters Francis Bacon (1909–92) and Lucian Freud (1922–2011); and contributor to the British 'pop art' movement, David Hockney (1937–).

THE TURNER PRIZE

In 2002, Labour politician Kim Howells and then junior minister at the Department for Culture, Media and Sport, described the Turner prize as 'conceptual bullshit'.

The most publicized and prestigious art award in the UK is the Turner Prize, named after the painter J. M. W. Turner and staged at the London art gallery Tate Britain. Often associated with conceptual art, past entries, which include Damien Hirst's 'Shark in Formaldehyde' and *My Bed* by Tracey Emin (which didn't actually win), have proved controversial. It has also spawned various other spoof prizes, to include the Turnip Prize, described as 'a crap art competition with judging criteria including "Lack of effort" and "Is it shit?"'.

Previous Turner Prize winners include: 2014, Duncan Campbell for his 'essay film' *It for Others*; 2013, Laure Prouvost for her film *Wantee*; 2012, Elizabeth Price for her video installation *The Woolworths Choir of 1979*; 2011, Martin Boyce for his installation *Do Words Have Voices*; 2010, Susan Philipsz for her aural installation *Lowlands Away*.

TV AND THE INTERNET

'People who watch morning television are elderly, infirm or emotionally immature.'

LABOUR POLITICIAN ROY HATTERSLEY

Watching TV is the most popular leisure activity in the UK. In 2010, British people watched an average of four hours two minutes every day compared with two hours fifty-three minutes listening to the radio. In Britain, 98 per cent of households own a TV, and in 2010, 10 million subscribed to BSkyB, Britain's biggest UK satellite broadcaster, and 4.2 million to cable TV.

In 2012, 33 million adults used the Internet every day (more than double the 2006 figure of 16 million), 48 per cent of all adults used social networking sites (87 per cent of adults aged between sixteen and twenty-four). Many people now use the Internet in preference to television.

Television is provided by terrestrial, cable and satellite broadcasters and is either free to view or payable through subscription. The most viewed channels are BBC One and Two, ITV, Channel 4/SFC and Channel 5.

In the UK, anyone with a TV, computer or any other medium used for watching television must obtain a TV licence. The fee is set annually by the British government and agreed by Parliament.

TV soap opera dramas, talent competition shows, sports events and coverage of royal events often top the viewing ratings in the UK.

THE BEEB

Founded in 1922, the BBC is the world's largest and oldest broadcaster, funded primarily by the television licence. It has several television channels, as well as ten national radio stations and forty-six regional and local radio stations. It also provides for a worldwide audience via the BBC World Service and is available in 150 capital cities. Around the world it is famed for its integrity and honest journalism and in the UK it is affectionately known as 'the Beeb' or 'Auntie'.

In 2012, the London Olympic Games delivered the biggest national television event since measuring systems began with 90 per cent of the UK population watching at least fifteen minutes of coverage. The opening ceremony attracted an average audience of 27.3 million and 20 million tuned in to watch Usain Bolt win the 100-metre final.

In 2011, more than 24 million viewers in the UK watched the royal wedding of Prince William and Catherine Middleton on the BBC and ITV, with more than 34 million viewers watching at least part of the royal wedding coverage during the day. (In the US, nearly 23 million people watched the ceremony.)

CLASSIC BRITISH TV AND FILM

Monty Python's Flying Circus

A surreal television comedy sketch show, *Monty Python's Flying Circus* aired on the BBC between 1969 and 1974 and significantly influenced absurdist comedy around the world, spawning books, stage shows and films (to include *Monty Python and the Holy Grail* and *Monty's Python's Life of Brian*). The Monty Python team included John Cleese, Terry Gilliam, Graham Chapman, Eric Idle, Terry Jones and Michael Palin.

THE SPANISH INQUISITION

Monty Python has become part of the modern lexicon of Britain, even entering the political arena. In October 2010, David Cameron opened his speech at the Tory party conference with 'They said we had ceased to be. That we were an ex-party. But it turns out we really were actually only resting.' And in 2010, when *Telegraph* journalist Matthew d'Ancona asked a cabinet minister whether he'd expected such a furore over child benefit proposals, he replied: 'Well, I certainly didn't expect the Spanish Inquisition.'

Doctor Who

The BBC science-fiction series *Doctor Who* has become a cult favourite in the UK, running from 1963 to 1989, and then relaunched by the writer Russell T. Davies in 2005 to great critical and popular success. With his various companions, the Doctor explores the universe in his time machine (which is known as the TARDIS, which stands for Time and Relative Dimension in Space), facing a variety of adversaries in the form of Daleks and Cybermen. The revived series is aired in around fifty countries around the world.

Mr Bean

A silent, oddball character, Mr Bean is known across the world. Starring Rowan Atkinson, the show originated as a fourteen-part series broadcast in 1990 and sold to 190 territories worldwide. The character was transformed into an animated series, two movies and made an appearance at the London 2012 Olympics.

Political figures in the UK have often been compared to Mr Bean – *Private Eye* magazine depicts current Labour leader Ed Miliband as Mr Bean in its cartoon strip, *The Adventures of Mr Milibean*. In a 2003 episode of *The Simpsons*, Homer mistakes the then prime minister Tony Blair for Mr Bean.

Charlie Chaplin

London-born Charlie Chaplin (1889–1977) has been regarded as one of the most important figures in film history. Producer, writer, composer and performer, Chaplin's most famous alter ego 'the little Tramp' turned him into the biggest star of the silent-movie era and many argue that no other comedian has matched his worldwide impact. Many of his films, which include *The Kid* (1921), *The Gold Rush* (1925), *Modern Times* (1936) and *The Great Dictator* (1940), are regarded as classics.

Carry On

The Carry On films were a sequence of British comedy films produced between 1958 and 1992 that were often panned by the critics but loved by British audiences. Dreadful puns, innuendo and slapstick were the hallmarks of the series and reminiscent of the music-hall acts popular in the UK as well as saucy seaside postcards. All thirty-one films were churned out at a rapid rate and made at Pinewood Studios.

Wallace and Gromit

Cheese-enthusiast Wallace and his long-suffering dog Gromit are the animated stars of four short films and one feature film, *The Curse of the Were-Rabbit*. Popular around the world, the pair were described by Culture 24's ICONS project as 'doing more to improve the image of the English worldwide than any officially appointed ambassador'.

James Bond

Very much a British icon, James Bond was created by author Ian Fleming and brought to life in cinema's longest-running franchise film. Agent 007 of the British Secret Intelligence Service (MI6), the smooth super-spy, uses the latest gadgets to bring international gangsters to justice while inevitably bedding a host of beautiful women along the way. This iconic symbol of the UK appeared in the opening ceremony of the 2012 London Olympics as the escort of Queen Elizabeth II.

THE FILM INDUSTRY

Many of the world's highest-grossing movies are produced in Britain using British talent, although the films are funded by foreign companies. The James Bond and the Harry Potter franchises are huge box-office hits and are both produced in the UK. In 2013, the Bond movie *Skyfall* became the highest-grossing movie in the UK.

In 1999, the British Film Institute came up with 100 of the greatest British Films of the twentieth century. The top ten, with their directors, are:

1. *The Third Man* (1949) – Carol Reed
2. *Brief Encounter* (1945) – David Lean
3. *Lawrence of Arabia* (1962) – David Lean
4. *The 39 Steps* (1935) – Alfred Hitchcock
5. *Great Expectations* (1946) – David Lean
6. *Kind Hearts and Coronets* (1949) – Robert Hamer

7. *Kes* (1969) – Ken Loach
8. *Don't Look Now* (1973) – Nicolas Roeg
9. *The Red Shoes* (1948) – Powell and Pressburger
10. *Trainspotting* (1996) – Danny Boyle

SPORT

In Britain, sport plays an important part in many people's lives. In England during the year to April 2013, 15.3 million people played sport at least once a week. Many famous sports, including football, rugby and cricket, originated in Britain and the British are keen sports fans.

FOOTBALL

Britain is home to the oldest football league in the world and the oldest competition (the FA Cup), and its English Premier League is one of the richest sports leagues in the world, attracting a huge international audience and some of the best players from around the globe. England, Wales, Northern Ireland and Scotland have separate leagues, in which clubs representing different towns and cities compete against each other.

Organized football games, largely played at English schools, have been documented in the UK as far back as 1581. The world's oldest club, Sheffield Football Club, was formed in 1857, and in 1863 the modern game of football was first codified.

The FA Cup (the Football Association Challenge Cup) started in 1871. As of 2014, Manchester United and Arsenal have had the most FA Cup wins with eleven victories respectively, followed by Tottenham Hotspur with eight.

The Scottish Premier League (SPL) was founded in 1998. Since then, nineteen clubs participated, but Celtic, one of the Old Firm Glasgow clubs, continued to dominate the league, winning seven titles since the league's inception. It was dissolved in 2013 when it merged with the Scottish Football League to form the Scottish Professional Football League.

SPORTS FAN

During a radio interview in 2001, the BBC sports presenter Clare Balding pitched five questions to Richard Caborn, the new Labour Minister for Sport, on his chosen topics. He was asked to name the England cricket coach, the captain of the Lions rugby squad, three jockeys riding at Ascot, three European golfers playing in the US Open, and the four semi-finalists in the Stella Artois tennis championship. He failed to answer one correctly.

CRICKET

Played on village greens up and down the country, cricket is seen as the quintessential English sport. Club matches can last all day and professional matches as long as five days (with players breaking for lunch and tea), only to end in a draw. A complex system of laws dictate play, as does the English code of sportsmanship and fair play.

Test matches are held between international teams, in which two teams play a four-inning match. The most famous of these are a series of Test matches between England and Australia, known as the Ashes.

ASHES TO ASHES

The 'Ashes' name is taken from a mock obituary for English cricket published in the British newspaper *The Sporting Times* in 1882, after Australia had beaten England at the Oval for the first time. The article declared that English cricket had died and that its 'body will be cremated and the ashes taken to Australia'. Subsequent tours were then seen as a quest to recover the ashes.

The English cricket team represents England and Wales. Scotland and Ireland both have cricket teams but they do not have Test status and the sport has a much lower profile.

RUGBY

Legend has it that rugby was founded in 1823 when Rugby School pupil William Webb Ellis picked up the ball during a game of association football and ran towards the goal. There is no actual historical evidence for this story, although the first rules of the game were written at Rugby School in 1843. The sport is popular throughout the UK with two types of rugby played, Rugby Union and Rugby League, each with different rules, teams and leagues. The Six Nations Championship is one of the most famous Rugby Union competitions, played between England, France, Ireland (representing the Republic of Ireland and Northern Ireland), Wales, Scotland and Italy. England won the Rugby World Cup in 2003.

TENNIS

The popular sport of tennis was also founded in England, specifically in Birmingham, in the late nineteenth century. Wimbledon (formally called 'The Championships, Wimbledon') is the oldest tennis tournament in the world and the only major tournament to be played on grass.

A TASTY TREAT

Strawberries and cream are traditionally eaten at Wimbledon, a custom started by King George V (1865–1936) who ate them while watching a game. In the 2012 tournament, 142,000 portions of strawberries were sold. Also, players ate 12,000 bananas and 54,000 Slazenger balls were used during the fortnight.

MOTOR RACING

Britain has a strong tradition of motor racing, with the majority of Formula One teams based in England. The first F1 Grand Prix was held at Silverstone in 1950, where the British Grand Prix is held every year. Formula One world title holders include: Graham Hill (1962 and 1968), Jackie Stewart (1969, 1971 and 1973), James Hunt (1976), Nigel Mansell (1992), Damon Hill (Graham Hill's son, 1996), Lewis Hamilton (2008 and 2014) and Jenson Button (2009).

GOLF

The famous St Andrews golf course in Scotland is generally regarded as the 'home of golf', and the modern game of golf can indeed be traced back to fifteenth-century Scotland (when James II banned the game as an unwelcome distraction from archery). The Open Championship is played each summer in the UK (mostly on Scottish courses) and it is the oldest of the major golf tournaments. Top golfers include Northern Ireland's Rory McIlroy, England's Justin Rose, Lee Westwood and Nick Faldo, Scotland's Colin Montgomerie and Wales's Ian Woosnam.

HORSE RACING

After football, the second largest spectator sport in the UK is horse racing with more than 5.7 million people in 2009 going to the races. Newmarket in Suffolk is seen as the home of British racing and the UK is a major centre for thoroughbred horse breeding – of the current top ten-rated horses in the world, six were trained in Great Britain. There are two main forms of racing – flat racing and national hunt racing (over hurdles or jumps) – and major horse-racing events include Royal Ascot, the Epsom Derby, the Grand National and the Cheltenham Gold Cup. Gambling and horse racing have a strong tradition in the UK, with the gross profits of all bets taxed by the government.

KEY BRITISH SPORTING EVENTS
YOU SHOULD KNOW

6 May 1954 Roger Bannister becomes the first man in the world to run a mile in less than four minutes (3 minutes 59.4 seconds) at Iffley Road Track in Oxford.

20 July 1966 The FIFA World Cup final. The host nation, England (captained by Bobby Moore), beats West Germany 4–2 at Wembley Stadium, winning the World Cup for the first time. Geoff Hurst scores a hat-trick of goals (in the nineteenth minute and twice again in extra time) with Martin Peters scoring the second goal in the seventy-eighth minute. Debate has long since raged over Hurst's second goal, after his shot hit the crossbar and bounced onto the goal line, with some believing the ball didn't cross the line.

BBC reporter Kenneth Wolstenholme's commentary for Hurst's third goal in the closing minutes of the game – 'Some people are on the pitch. They think it's all over... [Hurst scores] It is now!' – is now the most celebrated commentary in sports-broadcasting history.

14 February 1984 At the Winter Olympic Games, which were held in Sarajevo, Bosnia-Herzegovina (then Yugoslavia), British ice dancers Jayne Torvill and Christopher Dean receive the highest ever scores for a single programme with twelve out of eighteen possible sixes for their sensuous dance performance of Ravel's 'Bolero'.

23 September 2000 At the Sydney Olympic Games, British rower Steven Redgrave wins his fifth gold medal, this time in the coxless pair event.

23 and 28 August 2004 At the Athens Olympic Games, athlete Kelly Holmes wins two gold medals for the 800-metre and 1,500-metre events and holds numerous British and European records.

7 February 2005 Yachtswoman Ellen MacArthur becomes the fastest person to circumnavigate the globe single-handed.

8–28 August 2008 The Beijing Olympics, at which track cyclist Chris Hoy wins three gold medals and British Paralympian swimmer Ellie Simmonds, who at thirteen was the youngest member of the British team, wins two gold medals in the freestyle events.

22 July 2012 Cyclist Bradley Wiggins becomes the first ever British winner of the Tour de France.

'They are like glistening wet otters frolicking.'

MAYOR OF LONDON BORIS JOHNSON ON WOMEN'S BEACH
VOLLEYBALL AT THE 2012 LONDON OLYMPIC GAMES,
THE TELEGRAPH, 31 JULY 2012.

1 August 2012 Bradley Wiggins wins gold in the cycling time trial at the London Olympics. With a total of seven gold medals, Wiggins shares the record with Chris Hoy for most decorated British Olympian (see on page 232).

3 August 2012 Chris Hoy and Great Britain's team sprint squad win gold in the men's final.

4 August 2012 Track-and-field athlete Jessica Ennis takes the gold in the heptathlon with a British and European record score of points at the Olympic Games. Athlete Mo Farah wins Britain's first ever gold medal in the 10,000-metre race. Farah is noted for his victory pose, 'the Mobot'.

7 August 2012 Chris Hoy wins his sixth Olympic medal at the Olympic Games. With six gold medals and one silver medal, he is, with cyclist Bradley Wiggins, the most decorated British Olympian.

11 August 2012 Mo Farah wins gold in the 5,000-metre race at the Olympic Games.

1 September 2012 Ellie Simmonds takes her first gold at the 2012 Paralympic Games. She takes her second gold on 4 September.

10 September 2012 Following his gold medal win at the London Olympics, tennis player Andy Murray beats Novak Djokovic in the final of the US Open to become the first British man since 1936 to win a grand-slam title.

7 July 2013 Andy Murray becomes the first British male in seventy-seven years to win the Wimbledon Championships.

THE ISLES OF WONDER

The opening ceremony of the 2012 London Olympic Games, entitled 'Isles of Wonder' and directed by British film director Danny Boyle, was generally regarded as a huge success, with the *Daily Telegraph* saying it was 'brilliant, breathtaking, bonkers and utterly British'. Reception overseas was generally very positive with the Chinese news agency Zinhua describing the ceremony as an 'eccentric and exuberant celebration of British history, art and culture'. Back in the UK, some on the political right viewed the ceremony, with its portrayal of the NHS, grime music and multicultural families, as left-wing propaganda or, as Conservative MP Aidan Burley described it on Twitter, 'leftie multicultural crap'. Boris Johnson swiftly dismissed his claims as 'nonsense' and David Cameron later said that it was an 'idiotic thing to say'.

At the end of the 'green and pleasant land' sequence, the Victorian engineer Isambard Kingdom Brunel, played by Kenneth Branagh, delivers Caliban's 'Be not afeard' speech from Shakespeare's *The Tempest* (Act 3, Scene II). The speech signifies a new era in Britain and the next sequence of the ceremony, which ushers in Industrial Britain.

233

NATIONAL CUISINE

'I love England, especially the food. There's nothing
I like more than a lovely bowl of pasta'.

NAOMI CAMPBELL, 2006.

FISH AND CHIPS

Fish and chips is the most popular takeaway food in Great Britain, with around 11,500 fish and chip shops across the country. Each year the British consume over 250 million servings of fish and chips, and one in six Brits goes to a 'chippie' at least once a week. On a Friday, 20 per cent of meals in Britain are bought in a fish and chip shop (known as a 'fish supper' in Northern Ireland and Scotland), and in the country as a whole, one in three potatoes ends up as a chip.

Most UK chippies coat their fish – usually cod, haddock, pollock or other types of white fish – with a simple water-and-flour batter. In Wales, Northern Ireland and northern England many chippies serve the side sauces of gravy and curry sauce.

The expansion of trawl fishing in the North Sea and the development of railways connecting ports to major cities led to the increasing popularity of fish and chips as a major stock meal for the working classes. Chip shops opened in northern England throughout the nineteenth century, the first recorded fish and chip shop opening in London in 1860, and the great Victorian novelist Charles

Dickens mentioned a 'fried fish' warehouse in *Oliver Twist*, first published in 1837, the year Queen Victoria came to the throne. In the following century, during and after the Second World War, fish and chips remained one of the few foods not subject to rationing, although supplies of fish were often limited, and people complained of sub-standard chips because of the poor-quality fat available.

A BIT ON THE SIDE

'Can I have a pot of that nice avocado mousse?' – A reported remark by the then Labour MP Peter Mandelson (now Lord Mandelson) as he pointed to mushy peas in a fish and chip shop in his Hartlepool constituency, in 2008. (He denies having said this.)

Mushy peas are traditionally served with the popular British staple, fish and chips. They are made from marrowfat peas (a matured, dried form of the garden pea), which are combined with water, sugar and salt to form a thick, green, lumpy soup – the taste of which bears little resemblance to guacamole.

Mushy peas are particularly associated with northern England, where they are sometimes served as part of the snack 'pie and peas'. In upmarket restaurants they are occasionally referred to as 'Yorkshire caviar'.

INDIAN AND CHINESE CUISINE

Almost as popular as fish and chips are oriental and Indian cuisines (or at least a British version of them).

The man behind the Chinese takeaway was John Koon, the proprietor of the Cathay Restaurant near Piccadilly Circus, who in the 1950s introduced the 'A, B, C' set menu to his British customers. He also convinced entrepreneur Billy Butlin to open kitchens in his Butlin's holiday camps with a simple but hugely popular menu of chicken chop suey and chips.

THE FULL ENGLISH BREAKFAST

Somerset Maugham once said: 'To eat well in England you should have breakfast three times a day.' While this isn't a great endorsement for other types of British food, the full English breakfast, which usually consists of bacon, sausages, eggs and a bit of fried toast thrown in, is regarded as a staple of English cuisine (and as a cure for the worst hangovers). It is usually used to differentiate from the European continental-style breakfast. In Northern Ireland, an 'Ulster fry' is similar to a full English, with the addition of soda bread and potato bread, and white or black pudding.

THE SUNDAY ROAST

The British love their Sunday roasts, which usually consist of roasted meat with potatoes and vegetables, covered in gravy. The most British of meats is beef (so much so that the French call us 'rosbifs', see page 14) although chicken, lamb and pork are also popular. Yorkshire puddings (batter baked in the oven) are also served as an accompaniment. The tradition for Sunday roasts dates back centuries (although some claim it dates back to Yorkshire in the Industrial Revolution) – when the meat could be left roasting in the oven while families attended church, and the leftovers eaten cold during the week.

MARMITE

A product largely unknown in large parts of the world, Marmite is a sticky dark-brown food-spread made from yeast extract, first manufactured in 1902 in Burton, Staffordshire, fed from excess yeast at the Bass Brewery. The British have a love/hate relationship with the distinctive, powerful flavour of Marmite (as reflected in its 'love it or hate it' marketing campaign), while foreigners often regard it with something close to abhorrence – the American author Bill Bryson describes it as 'an edible yeast extract with the visual properties of an industrial lubricant'. April 2012 saw the release of a special Diamond Jubilee edition with the product renamed 'Ma'amite'.

PASTYGATE

'… I am a pasty-eater myself. I go to Cornwall on holiday. I love a hot pasty. I think the last one I bought was from the West Cornwall Pasty Company. I seem to remember I was in Leeds station at the time and the choice was whether to have one of their small ones or large ones, and I have a feeling I opted for the large one and very good it was too.'

Prime Minister David Cameron, quoted on 28 March 2012 during the controversy over VAT at 20 per cent being charged on all food sold 'above ambient temperature'. The issue became a political controversy, dubbed by some in the press as 'pastygate', because it later emerged that the West Cornwall Pasty Company outlet in Leeds station had shut down several years before the PM claimed he had eaten the pasty. When George Osborne was asked by Labour MP John Mann when he'd last had a Cornish pasty, he answered that he had no idea when he had last eaten one, leading some in the press to claim that the Conservative Party were 'out of touch' with the ordinary man.

HAGGIS

Haggis is a traditional Scottish dish in which offal, suet, onions and oatmeal are encased in a sheep's stomach or sausage casing. It is often served with 'neeps and tatties' (turnip and potato).

TEA AND CREAM TEAS

Afternoon tea is one of the most quintessential of British customs, with tea drinking first popularized by King Charles II and his Portuguese wife Catherine De Braganza in the 1660s. It is said that taking tea in the afternoon wasn't introduced until as late as the nineteenth century, introduced by the Duchess of Bedford in 1840 who began to invite friends round for tea at around 4 p.m. A cream tea consists of tea, scones, clotted cream and jam, and is associated with Devon and Cornwall, although it is sold throughout the country.

ALCOHOL

The Brits like to drink, and also, like other northern Europeans from colder climes, to drink to excess. This passion for alcohol is a time-honoured tradition, stretching at least back to the medieval period when proverbs remarked, 'The Norman sings, the German guzzles, the Englishman boozes'. As water wasn't deemed safe to drink at this time, by the 1600s beer had become the liquid staple of our diet – even for women and children, who drank a particularly weak version, known as small beer. In the 1700s gin began to rival beer as the most popular drink and drunkenness became so widespread that the government was forced to pass the 1751 Gin Act in a bid to reduce the consumption of the so-called 'Mother's ruin'.

Today, binge drinking is still a common pastime in the UK and is more widespread among British teenagers than in most other Western countries. In 2013, the *European Journal of Public Health* estimated that three-quarters of people in England exceed the recommended limits of alcohol on their heaviest drinking day.

In 2011, there were 8,748 alcohol-related deaths in the UK, and over 66 per cent of all alcohol-related deaths in the UK in 2011 were among males.

The Royal College of Physicians recommend weekly alcohol limits of twenty-one units for men and fourteen units for women. The UK Chief Medical Officers have recommended not to regularly exceed 3–4 units per day for men (equivalent in total to a pint and a half of 4 per cent beer) and 2–3 units a day for women (equivalent to a 175 ml glass of wine).

BINGE DRINKER

In an interview with GQ magazine in August 2000, the then leader of the Conservative Party William Hague said that as a teenager, when doing a summer job delivering drinks to pubs across South Yorkshire, he drank fourteen pints a day. 'We used to have a pint at every stop and we used to have about fourteen stops a day,' he said.

In his hometown of Rotherham, people met this with scepticism: 'The idea of him sinking fourteen pints a day is laughable – nobody has seen him round here for years.' PR man Max Clifford said the claim was an attempt by Hague to shed his image as a fusty political youth: 'It won't work because it is obvious – you don't look at him and see a fourteen-pint man.'

THE ENGLISH LANGUAGE

One of Britain's biggest exports is its language. An estimated one-quarter of the world can speak English to some degree and it is the third most common native language in the world after Mandarin Chinese and Spanish.

A working knowledge of English is required in many fields and professions, to include medicine and technology and science; three-quarters of the world's mail is written in English and four-fifths of all data stored on computer is in English. It is also the dominant language of international diplomacy and the official language of the European Union, United Nations and many world organizations.

GOBBLEDEGOOK AND POLITICIAN SPEAK

'Since becoming a Member of Parliament I've been learning a new language ... No one ever uses a simple Anglo-Saxon word, or a concrete example, where a Latinate construction or a next-to-meaningless abstraction can be found.'

CONSERVATIVE MP AND EDUCATION SECRETARY MICHAEL GOVE IN *THE TIMES*, 8 DECEMBER 2008.

Politicians, officials and institutions frequently slip into empty jargon or insincere clichés to dress up simple ideas or, as George Orwell put it, 'give an appearance of solidity to pure wind'. This kind of political spin disguises unpalatable truths, such as staff or budget cuts, which can be redefined as 'downsizing', 'realignment of resources' or 'efficiency savings'. All too often clarity and simplicity are replaced by long-winded legalese and pretentious gobbledegook – much of which builds barriers between government or officials and the public.

BOOK OF BOLLOCKS

Labour MP Tessa Jowell said in 2004 that she kept a 'little book of bollocks' containing instances of government jargon and gobbledegook:

'The risk is when you have been in government for eight years you begin to talk the language, which is not the language of the real world.'

TESSA JOWELL SPEAKING TO THE *FINANCIAL TIMES*, 23 DECEMBER 2004.

Organizations, like the Plain English Campaign, oppose and expose this kind of gobbledegook, jargon and legalese in favour of clear, plain English in all public communication.

The Plain English Campaign presents each year the 'Foot in Mouth Award' for 'a baffling comment by a public figure'. Politicians have won the award more than any other type of person (although sports figures have won it four times) with the Cardiff politician Rhodri Morgan winning it twice.

Morgan won his first award in 1998 after an appearance on BBC's *Newsnight*, when he answered Jeremy Paxman's question on whether he would like to be the Labour leader of the new Welsh Assembly with, 'Does a one-legged duck swim in circles?' Paxman paused for a long while and asked whether that was Welsh for 'yes'?

Morgan's second award came in 2005 after his comment on policing: 'The only thing which isn't up for grabs is no change and I think it's fair to say, it's all to play for, except for no change.'

Other winners include:

England manager Steve McClaren, who in 2007 on Radio 5 Live described footballer Wayne Rooney as 'inexperienced, but he's experienced in terms of what he's been through'.

Conservative MP and current Mayor of London Boris Johnson who in 2004 on BBC's *Have I Got News for You* said: 'I could not fail to disagree with you less.'

AT THE END OF THE DAY

According to a 2004 survey conducted by the Plain English Campaign, the most annoying clichés in the English language are:

1. 'At the end of the day'
2. 'At this moment in time'
3. The constant use of 'like'
4. 'With all due respect'

Other annoying clichés include: '24/7', 'address the issue', 'ballpark figure', 'going forward', 'ongoing', 'pushing the envelope', 'thinking outside the box', 'touch base', 'value-added'.

PREPOSITIONS

'"If" is a very large preposition.'

CONSERVATIVE MP JOHN MAJOR IN 1990.

'If' is of course not a preposition, which is a word that normally precedes a noun or pronoun, telling you where or when something happened, as in 'the man *on* the street' and 'she arrived *after* lunch'. There is a traditional view that prepositions should not come at the end of sentences, although this can often result in awkward, unnatural-sounding sentences and it is now widely accepted. Winston Churchill famously opposed the ruling, saying, 'This is the sort of English *up with* which I will not put.'

SELECTED BIBLIOGRAPHY

BOOKS

A Miscellany of Britain by Tom O'Meara (Arcturus Publishing, 2007)

Adventures on the High Teas: In Search of Middle England by Stuart Maconie (Ebury Press, 2010)

Bad Language: The Use and Abuse of Official Language (report by House of Commons Select Committee available on parliament.uk, 30 November 2009)

British Civilization: An Introduction by John Oakland (Routledge, 2011)

Classic Political Clangers by David Mortimer (Robson Books, 2006)

DK Eyewitness Travel Guide: Great Britain by Michael Leapman (Dorling Kindersley, 2011)

I Used to Know That: History by Emma Marriott (Michael O'Mara, 2010)

Life in the UK Test Study Guide (Red Squirrel Publishing, 2012)

Life in the United Kingdom: A Guide for New Residents (The Stationery Office, 2013)

Life in the United Kingdom: A Journey to Citizenship (The Stationery Office, 2007)

Mission Accomplished: Things Politicians Wish They Hadn't Said by Matthew Paris and Phil Mason (JR Books, 2007)

Notes From a Small Island by Bill Bryson (Black Swan, 1996)

Pocket Companion Guide to Political Quotations by Caroline Rathbone and Michael Stephenson (Longman Group, 1985)

The English: A Portrait of a People by Jeremy Paxman (Michael Joseph, 1998)

The Oxford Dictionary of Political Quotations by Antony Jay (Oxford University Press, 2012)

The Usborne History of Britain by Ruth Brocklehurst (Usborne Publishing)

They Got It Wrong! The Guinness Dictionary of Regrettable Quotations by David Milsted (Guinness Publishing, 1998)

WEBSITES

avert.org/uk
basc.org.uk
bbc.co.uk
environment-agency.gov.uk
fullfact.org
gov.uk
guardian.co.uk
homeoffice.gov.uk
independent.co.uk
ipsos-mori.com
lawontheweb.co.uk
ons.gov.uk
parliament.uk
plainenglish.co.uk
ramblers.org.uk
royal.gov.uk
salvationarmy.org
standard.co.uk
telegraph.co.uk
thetimes.co.uk
totalpolitics.com
ukpolitical.info
wimbledon.com

INDEX

(page numbers in italics refer to illustrations)